3

כָּל יִשְׂרָאֵל

The Prayers of Our People

By Gila Gevirtz

Activities:

Ellen J. Rank

Editorial Committee:

Rabbi Martin S. Cohen

Rabbi William Cutter

Sarah Gluck

Dina Maiben

Behrman House, Inc.

www.behrmanhouse.com

www.kolyisrael.net

Contents

4   (1) אֵין כָּמוֹךְ/אַב הָרַחֲמִים

14   (2) כִּי מִצִּיּוֹן/בָּרוּךְ שֶׁנָּתַן/שְׁמַע/ גַּדְלוּ לַיְיָ/לְךָ יְיָ

26   (3) בִּרְכוֹת הַתּוֹרָה

38   (4) בִּרְכוֹת הַהַפְטָרָה

52   (5) עָלֵינוּ

60   (6) קַדִּישׁ

70   (7) אֵין כֵּאלֹהֵינוּ/אֲדוֹן עוֹלָם

84   Kol Yisrael Wrap-Up

94   מִלּוֹן

For Hannah, Laili, and Jacob; Ben, Noah, Simon, and Eve. — G.G.

The publisher gratefully acknowledges the cooperation of the following sources of photographs for this book: Creative Image 35, 48, 61; Friends of Israel Scouts, Inc. 58; Gila Gevirtz 44; Terry S. Kaye 11 (right), 40, 47, 49, 76; Richard Lobell 29, 87; Dena Neusner 75; Hannah E. Pasternak 11 (left); Varina and Jay Patel/123rf 67; Ginny Twersky 20

Book and cover design: Stacey May
Illustration: Pamela Hamilton (cover and story art), Marc Monés (activity art)
Project Editor: Terry S. Kaye

יִשְׂרָאֵל

Use this map as your guide as you travel around Israel with Ben and Batya.

B en and Batya were bursting with excitement. Their parents had received a research grant in medical nanotechnology from the Hebrew University of Jerusalem. Now the family was flying to Israel for the year. As the El Al jet landed at Ben Gurion International Airport, the twins eagerly anticipated the adventures that lay ahead—going to a new school, learning to speak Hebrew, and making new friends. But their top priority was finding a site in Israel for the biggest event of the year—their bar and bat mitzvah celebration. ▪▪

Describe an event that you are looking forward to, like a trip or becoming a bar or bat mitzvah.

_____

_____

In what ways does the anticipation add to your excitement?

_____

_____

Judaism's teachings and traditions stem from the Torah. So it is no surprise that the highlight and heart of the שַׁבָּת morning prayer service is the reading of the weekly Torah portion—פָּרָשַׁת הַשָּׁבוּעַ. The prayers and songs leading up to the Torah service are designed to heighten our anticipation. You will learn about the first two prayers—אֵין כָּמוֹךָ and אַב הָרַחֲמִים—in this chapter. Although these prayers help prepare our hearts and minds to receive the words of Torah, it is God, not the Torah, they praise.

Why do you think we praise God rather than the Torah?

The Torah Service

Most congregations read from the Torah on שַׁבָּת morning and on certain Jewish holidays. Other congregations read from the Torah on Friday evening—עֶרֶב שַׁבָּת. Some also read from the Torah on Shabbat afternoons, and on Mondays and Thursday mornings.

✈ **Torah Travel** Communal readings of the Torah began nearly 2,500 years ago in Jerusalem—יְרוּשָׁלַיִם—where Ezra, a Jewish religious leader and scribe, read from the Torah at public gatherings on Mondays, Thursdays, Shabbat, and on certain holidays...

וַיָּבִיא עֶזְרָא ... אֶת־הַתּוֹרָה לִפְנֵי הַקָּהָל ... וַיִּקְרָא־בּוֹ

"Ezra brought ... the Torah before the gathering...and read from it."

(Nehemiah 8:2–3)

Why on Mondays and Thursdays? That was when many people gathered in the marketplace to do business. Locate and circle Jerusalem on the map on page 3.

אֵין כָּמוֹךָ

The first part of the Torah service—taking the Torah out of the Ark—begins with אֵין כָּמוֹךָ. It describes God as the eternal Ruler of the Jews. It also helps set the stage for us to receive the Torah, as if we ourselves were at Mount Sinai with Moses.

Practice reading אֵין כָּמוֹךָ.

1. אֵין כָּמוֹךָ בָאֱלֹהִים אֲדֹנָי, וְאֵין כְּמַעֲשֶׂיךָ.
2. מַלְכוּתְךָ מַלְכוּת כָּל־עֹלָמִים, וּמֶמְשַׁלְתְּךָ בְּכָל־דֹּר וָדֹר.
3. יְיָ מֶלֶךְ, יְיָ מָלָךְ, יְיָ יִמְלֹךְ לְעֹלָם וָעֶד.
4. יְיָ עֹז לְעַמּוֹ יִתֵּן, יְיָ יְבָרֵךְ אֶת עַמּוֹ בַשָּׁלוֹם.

1. *There is none like You among the gods [other people worship], Adonai, and there are no deeds like Yours.*
2. *Your sovereignty is an eternal sovereignty, and Your reign is from generation to generation.*
3. *Adonai is Ruler, Adonai ruled, Adonai will rule forever and ever.*
4. *May Adonai give strength to God's people, may Adonai bless God's people with peace.*

Prayer Words

Practice reading these words from אֵין כָּמוֹךָ.

(there is) none	אֵין
like You	כָּמוֹךָ
Your sovereignty	מַלְכוּתְךָ
from generation to generation	בְּכָל־דֹּר וָדֹר
strength	עֹז

Word Association

Next to each illustration, write the appropriate Hebrew prayer word(s) or phrase.

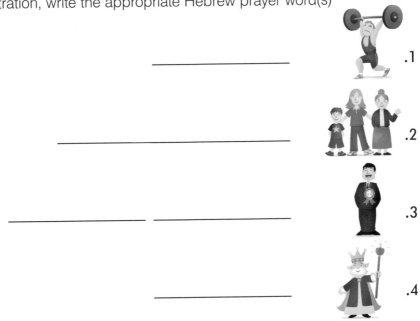

_____ .1

_____ .2

_____ _____ .3

_____ .4

Now match these words from אֵין כָּמוֹךָ in the column on the right to a related phrase from the siddur on the left.

כְּבוֹד מַלְכוּתְךָ	אֵין
לְדוֹר וָדוֹר	כָּמוֹךָ
אֵין כֵּאלֹהֵינוּ	מַלְכוּתְךָ
וְלוֹ הָעֹז וְהַמִּשְׂרָה	בְּכָל־דֹּר וָדֹר
מִי כָמֹכָה	עֹז

6

 **At the Root**

אֵין כָּמוֹךָ speaks of God as a מֶלֶךְ, which means ruler or king (sometimes translated as **sovereign**).

The root of מֶלֶךְ is מלכ.

The root מלכ tells us that **ruler** or **king** is part of a word's meaning.

God is sometimes called יְיָ מֶלֶךְ. Fill in the missing English translation:

Adonai (is) _____

Reread אֵין כָּמוֹךָ on page 5 and circle the words that are built on the root מלכ.

How many words did you circle? _____

The suffix ךָ means **you** or **your**. Write the word in line 2 of אֵין כָּמוֹךָ that is built on the root מלכ and ends with the suffix meaning **your**. _____

How many other words in line 2 end with the suffix meaning **you** or **your**? _____

Practice reading the following prayer phrases. Draw a crown above each word that has **ruler** or **king** as part of its meaning. Put a check next to the phrases in which God is called יְיָ מֶלֶךְ.

1. וַיֵּשֶׁב יְיָ מֶלֶךְ לְעוֹלָם

2. וְעֵינֵינוּ תִרְאֶינָה מַלְכוּתֶךָ

3. בָּרוּךְ שֵׁם כְּבוֹד מַלְכוּתוֹ לְעוֹלָם וָעֶד

4. יְיָ מֶלֶךְ לְעוֹלָם וָעֶד

5. יִשְׂמְחוּ בְמַלְכוּתֶךָ שׁוֹמְרֵי שַׁבָּת

6. וְהָיָה יְיָ לְמֶלֶךְ עַל כָּל הָאָרֶץ

אַב הָרַחֲמִים

The first part of the Torah service continues with אַב הָרַחֲמִים. This prayer describes God as a merciful parent and trustworthy ruler. It also asks for God's protection over Jerusalem. Practice reading אַב הָרַחֲמִים.

1. אַב הָרַחֲמִים, הֵיטִיבָה בִרְצוֹנְךָ אֶת צִיּוֹן;
2. תִּבְנֶה חוֹמוֹת יְרוּשָׁלָיִם.
3. כִּי בְךָ לְבַד בָּטָחְנוּ, מֶלֶךְ אֵל רָם וְנִשָּׂא,
4. אֲדוֹן עוֹלָמִים.

1. *Merciful Parent, favor Zion with Your goodness;*
2. *rebuild the walls of Jerusalem.*
3. *For in You alone do we trust, sovereign God, high and exalted,*
4. *eternal Ruler.*

 ## At the Root

The root of הָרַחֲמִים is רחם.

The root רחם tells us that **mercy** or **compassion** is part of a word's meaning.

God is sometimes called אַב הָרַחֲמִים. Fill in the missing English translation:

_____ Parent

Here are three other names by which God is known. Circle the root letters רחם in each phrase.

אֵל מָלֵא רַחֲמִים   אֵל רַחוּם וְחַנּוּן   הָרַחֲמָן

God Full of Mercy   Compassionate and   The Merciful One
                         Gracious God

Why do you think Judaism emphasizes that God is merciful? _____

_____

Prayer Words

Practice reading these words from אַב הָרַחֲמִים.

parent, father	אַב, אָב
merciful, the mercy	הָרַחֲמִים
walls	חוֹמוֹת
and exalted	וְנִשָּׂא
eternal	עוֹלָמִים

It's Our Motto

Write the English meaning next to each Hebrew word. Then copy the boxed letters to find the missing word below.

P _ _ _ _ [ ]   .1 אַב

_ _ _ [ ] _ _ _   .2 עוֹלָמִים

_ _ _ _ _ [ ] _   .3 הָרַחֲמִים

_ _ _ [ ] _ _   .4 חוֹמוֹת

_ _ _ _ _ [ ] _ _ _   .5 וְנִשָּׂא

The motto of the United States is: In God we _ _ _ _ _
                                                 1   2   3   4   5

Bonus Points: Write the word in line 3 of אַב הָרַחֲמִים on page 8 that means **we trust**.

Hint: The root letters are בטח.

_ _ _ _ _

🔗 Language Link

Zion—צִיּוֹן —is another name for Jerusalem—יְרוּשָׁלַיִם. Sometimes, צִיּוֹן refers only to Jerusalem and sometimes to the entire land of Israel—אֶרֶץ יִשְׂרָאֵל. Almost 2,000 years ago, Israel was conquered and our people went into exile.

Many prayers speak lovingly of Jerusalem, the capital of ancient Israel. In 1948 the Jewish people established the modern State of Israel—מְדִינַת יִשְׂרָאֵל—and today Jerusalem is once again Israel's thriving capital.

Below are the lyrics to Israel's national anthem, הַתִּקְוָה. It expresses our people's undying hope of returning from exile to live in our homeland.

Practice reading הַתִּקְוָה.

1. *Within the heart*	1. כָּל עוֹד בַּלֵּבָב פְּנִימָה
2. *the spirit of the Jew is still alive,*	2. נֶפֶשׁ יְהוּדִי הוֹמִיָּה,
3. *and the eyes look eastward*	3. וּלְפַאֲתֵי מִזְרָח קָדִימָה
4. *toward Zion.*	4. עַיִן לְצִיּוֹן צוֹפִיָּה.
5. *Our hope is not lost,*	5. עוֹד לֹא אָבְדָה תִּקְוָתֵנוּ,
6. *the hope of two thousand years*	6. הַתִּקְוָה בַּת שְׁנוֹת אַלְפַּיִם
7. *to be a free nation in our land,*	7. לִהְיוֹת עַם חָפְשִׁי בְּאַרְצֵנוּ,
8. *the land of Zion and Jerusalem.*	8. אֶרֶץ צִיּוֹן וִירוּשָׁלַיִם.

Circle the words צִיּוֹן and יְרוּשָׁלַיִם each time they appear in הַתִּקְוָה. How many words did you circle? _____

The Israel Connection

Love of Israel—אַהֲבַת צִיּוֹן—is a key Jewish value. Along with our commitment to the teachings of the Torah, אַהֲבַת צִיּוֹן plays a role in strengthening Jewish identity. Today, for example, we can show אַהֲבַת צִיּוֹן by going on a teen trip to Israel, learning to speak Hebrew, and marching in an Israel Day parade.

Suggest two other ways to show אַהֲבַת צִיּוֹן.

_____

How might these activities strengthen your Jewish identity?

_____

Pick the Pix

Below are two typical photos of Israel. Which do you think best illustrates the country?

Why did you make that choice?

_____

_____

אֶרֶץ צִיּוֹן וִירוּשָׁלַיִם

Reroll the Scroll

The תּוֹרָה is divided into 54 portions—פָּרָשׁוֹת. Each Shabbat we read a portion—פָּרָשָׁה—in synagogue. It takes one full year to complete our reading of the תּוֹרָה. And, as soon as we finish, on the holiday of שִׂמְחַת תּוֹרָה, we roll the scroll back to the beginning and start over again.

The ancient sage Ben Bag-Bag (yes, that's his name!) taught:

הֲפֹךְ בָּהּ וַהֲפֵךְ בָּהּ...

Turn it [the Torah] again and again, for everything is in it; think about it...
(Pirke Avot 5:25)

Explain what you think Ben Bag-Bag meant.

_____

_____

Why do *you* think we read the Torah, year after year, from our youth through old age?

_____

_____

Parashah Quiz

Read aloud the names of the first six פָּרָשׁוֹת in the Torah. Circle the פָּרָשָׁה that tells the story of Noah and the ark. Underline the פָּרָשָׁה that refers to our matriarch Sarah.

תּוֹלְדֹת　　חַיֵּי שָׂרָה　　וַיֵּרָא　　לֶךְ־לְךָ　　נֹחַ　　בְּרֵאשִׁית

Challenge: Copy the name of the פָּרָשָׁה that includes the story of creation AND is

the name of the first book of the Torah. _____

מַלְכוּתֶֽךָ   יִמְלֹךְ   מָלָךְ   מֶלֶךְ   מַלְכוּת   מַלְכוּתְךָ

Write the root on which these words are built. _____ _____ _____

Write the general meaning of these words. _____

Now choose the correct words from the list above to fill in the blanks. *Hint 1:* You will use one of the words twice. *Hint 2:* If you need help, turn to pages 5 and 8.

1. אֵין כָּמֽוֹךָ בָאֱלֹהִים אֲדֹנָי, וְאֵין כְּמַעֲשֶֽׂיךָ.

2. _____ _____ כָּל־עֹלָמִים, וּמֶמְשַׁלְתְּךָ בְּכָל־דֹּר וָדֹר.

3. יְיָ _____ , יְיָ _____ , יְיָ _____ לְעֹלָם וָעֶד.

4. יְיָ עֹז לְעַמּוֹ יִתֵּן, יְיָ יְבָרֵךְ אֶת עַמּוֹ בַשָּׁלוֹם.

5. אַב הָרַחֲמִים, הֵיטִֽיבָה בִרְצוֹנְךָ אֶת צִיּוֹן;

6. תִּבְנֶה חוֹמוֹת יְרוּשָׁלָֽיִם.

7. כִּי בְךָ לְבַד בָּטָֽחְנוּ, _____ אֵל רָם וְנִשָּׂא,

8. אֲדוֹן עוֹלָמִים.

Which word did you use twice? _____

Use this clue to complete the last board in the "Lion's Bird House" game in Level 1 on your computer.

"Israel is awesome." Batya said to Ben, several weeks after their arrival. "One moment we're in the Negev Desert walking the same paths as Abraham. The next we're seeing signs of the future—like the Negev's drip irrigation system. Did you know Israel is called the Silicon Valley of water technology?" ▆▆

✈️ **Torah Travel** Genesis 12:9 says: וַיִּסַּע אַבְרָם הָלוֹךְ וְנָסוֹעַ הַנֶּגְבָּה "Abram continued on his way toward the Negev." Locate and circle the Negev— נֶגֶב—on the map on page 3.

Which do you think would be more interesting, meeting Abraham in the Negev or meeting someone who lives in the future? Why? _____

_____

כִּי מִצִּיּוֹן, the prayer we recite as we remove the Torah from the Ark, provides yet another link in the age-old chain connecting our past and future. It honors the Land of Israel and the Torah as continuing sources of strength.

Why do you think the study of Torah—תַּלְמוּד תּוֹרָה—is an essential part of Jewish tradition?

_____

_____

כִּי מִצִּיּוֹן

The כִּי מִצִּיּוֹן prayer expresses our strong connection to the Torah and our hope that its lessons of justice and peace will spread throughout the world.

Below are three short quotes from the Torah (Leviticus 19). Choose one that you consider most important and give an example of how you apply it in your life today. Explain your choice.

Love your fellow human being as yourself.	1. וְאָהַבְתָּ לְרֵעֲךָ כָּמוֹךָ
Do not put a stumbling block before the blind.	2. וְלִפְנֵי עִוֵּר לֹא תִתֵּן מִכְשֹׁל
Leave them [the fallen fruits] for the poor.	3. לֶעָנִי וְלַגֵּר תַּעֲזֹב אֹתָם

_____

_____

Practice reading the כִּי מִצִּיּוֹן prayer.

1. For out of Zion shall go forth Torah,	1. כִּי מִצִּיּוֹן תֵּצֵא תוֹרָה,
2. and the word of God from Jerusalem.	2. וּדְבַר־יְיָ מִירוּשָׁלָיִם.

What do you think "the word of God" means?

_____

Prayer Variations

As the Ark is opened, some congregations say these words from the Torah (Numbers 10:35) before reciting כִּי מִצִּיּוֹן:

1. וַיְהִי בִּנְסֹעַ הָאָרֹן וַיֹּאמֶר מֹשֶׁה:

2. קוּמָה יְיָ וְיָפֻצוּ אֹיְבֶיךָ, וְיָנֻסוּ מְשַׂנְאֶיךָ מִפָּנֶיךָ.

1. When the Ark was carried forward, Moses said:
2. Arise, Adonai; may Your enemies be scattered, may Your foes be driven to flight.

Prayer Words

Practice reading these words from כִּי מִצִּיּוֹן.

out of Zion, from Zion	מִצִּיּוֹן
shall go forth	תֵּצֵא
from Jerusalem	מִירוּשָׁלָיִם

The Hills of Jerusalem

Jerusalem is a city of hills. Climb the hill below by circling, then reading, the Hebrew for each of the following English words or phrases. Remember to climb from line 1 to line 4.

1. shall go forth   2. from Zion   3. from Jerusalem   4. Torah

4. כִּי תּוֹרָה מִצִּיּוֹן תֵּצֵא
3. וּדְבַר־יְיָ מִצִּיּוֹן מִירוּשָׁלָיִם תֵּצֵא
2. כִּי תֵּצֵא תּוֹרָה מִצִּיּוֹן מִירוּשָׁלָיִם
1. תּוֹרָה מִצִּיּוֹן מִירוּשָׁלָיִם וּדְבַר־יְיָ תֵּצֵא

Now go down the hill by reading *all* the Hebrew words starting at the top.

 ## Be a Scribe

Torah scrolls are handwritten by highly trained scribes who use quill pens and black ink. Imagine that you are a scribe—סוֹפֵר. Complete the prayer by filling in the missing letters.

1. כִּי ＿ִצִּיּוֹן תֵּ＿א תוֹ＿ָ＿,
2. וּ＿ְ＿ַר־יְיָ מִ＿ ＿וּשָׁלָ＿ִם.

Putting It in ConTEXT

The words of כִּי מִצִּיּוֹן come from Isaiah 2:3. The next verse, Isaiah 2:4, introduces the prophet's vision of how there will be peace throughout the world when all nations follow ethical laws:

וְכִתְּתוּ חַרְבוֹתָם לְאִתִּים...
וַחֲנִיתוֹתֵיהֶם לְמַזְמֵרוֹת.
לֹא־יִשָּׂא גוֹי אֶל־גוֹי חֶרֶב
וְלֹא־יִלְמְדוּ עוֹד מִלְחָמָה.

...They shall beat their swords into plowshares
and their spears into pruning hooks.
Nation shall not raise sword against nation
and never again will they know war.

Describe what peace means to you. How does your vision compare to Isaiah's?

_____

_____

_____

At the Root

Part of the name יְרוּשָׁלַיִם is built on the root שׁלמ. Words that are built on שׁלמ have **wholeness** or **peace** as part of their meaning. In fact, Jerusalem is often called the "City of Peace."

Write the root letters of יְרוּשָׁלַיִם: _____ _____ _____ *Reminder:* ם *is a final* מ.

בָּרוּךְ שֶׁנָּתַן

The בָּרוּךְ שֶׁנָּתַן prayer helps us thank God for the gift of Torah.
Practice reading the בָּרוּךְ שֶׁנָּתַן blessing.

בָּרוּךְ שֶׁנָּתַן תּוֹרָה לְעַמּוֹ יִשְׂרָאֵל בִּקְדֻשָּׁתוֹ.

Praised is the One, who in holiness gave Torah to God's people Israel.

 **At the Root**

The root of בִּקְדֻשָּׁתוֹ is קדשׁ.
The root קדשׁ tells us that **set apart** or **separate** is part of a word's meaning.
Circle the Hebrew word in the בָּרוּךְ שֶׁנָּתַן blessing that is built on the root קדשׁ.

Now read the words a groom says to a bride under the ḥuppah:

הֲרֵי אַתְּ מְקֻדֶּשֶׁת לִי, בְּטַבַּעַת זוֹ, כְּדַת מֹשֶׁה וְיִשְׂרָאֵל.

*Behold, you are sanctified to me by this ring,
according to the laws of Moses and Israel.*

The bride might say:

הֲרֵי אַתָּה מְקֻדָּשׁ לִי, בְּטַבַּעַת זוֹ.

Behold, by this ring you are sanctified to me.

or

אֲנִי לְדוֹדִי וְדוֹדִי לִי.

I am my beloved's and my beloved is mine.

Read the following words aloud. Then circle the three root letters in each word.

וַיְקַדֵּשׁ   קָדוֹשׁ   קִדְּשָׁנוּ   קָדְשׁוֹ   מְקֻדֶּשֶׁת   הַקָּדוֹשׁ

This root has come to mean **holy**. What is the connection between **set apart** or
separate and **holy**?

_____

_____

Bonus Points: In the Hebrew words above circle the name of the blessing we
recite over wine.

Prayer Words

Practice reading these words from בָּרוּךְ שֶׁנָּתַן.

who gave, that gave	שֶׁנָּתַן
to God's people	לְעַמּוֹ
in (God's) holiness	בִּקְדֻשָׁתוֹ

To God's People

Look at the word לְעַמּוֹ.

לְ is a prefix meaning **to**.

וֹ at the end of a word means **his**.

עַם means **people** or **nation**. עַמּוֹ means **his people**.

As God is neither male nor female, we translate לְעַמּוֹ as **to God's people**.

Circle the word part that means **his** in the words below.

עַבְדוֹ   שְׁמוֹ   לְאוֹרוֹ   בִּקְדֻשָׁתוֹ   עַמּוֹ

The Gift of Torah

Each scroll contains words that are similar to one of the prayer words at the top of the page. Write that prayer word on the first blank line below the scroll. Then write its English meaning below that.

קִדְּשָׁנוּ
הַקֹּדֶשׁ

עַמְּךָ
עַם

נָתַתָּ
נוֹתֵן

_____   _____   _____

_____   _____   _____

Pledging Our Allegiance

In many congregations, after the Torah scroll—סֵפֶר תּוֹרָה—is taken out of the Ark, the person who holds it recites the two statements below—one at a time—first alone, then with the congregation. In other synagogues, everyone recites the lines in unison. These statements are like a pledge of allegiance to God.

Practice reading these lines.

וּ. שְׁמַע יִשְׂרָאֵל, יְיָ אֱלֹהֵינוּ, יְיָ אֶחָד.

1. Hear O Israel: Adonai is our God, Adonai is One.

2. אֶחָד אֱלֹהֵינוּ, גָּדוֹל אֲדוֹנֵנוּ, קָדוֹשׁ שְׁמוֹ.

2. Our God is One and is great; God's name is holy.

What is the name of the prayer on the first line above? Why do you think we recite it when we take the Torah out of the Ark?

_____

_____

Prayer Variations

Some congregations add a third line. The person holding the Torah scroll turns to face the Ark and bows while reciting this line.

גַּדְּלוּ לַיְיָ אִתִּי, וּנְרוֹמְמָה שְׁמוֹ יַחְדָּו.

Glorify Adonai with me, and together let us exalt God's name.

סֵפֶר תּוֹרָה

Prayer Words

Practice reading these words from גַּדְּלוּ לַיָי, and אֶחָד אֱלֹהֵינוּ, שְׁמַע יִשְׂרָאֵל.

one	אֶחָד
(God's) name, his name	שְׁמוֹ
glorify	גַּדְּלוּ

Odd Word Out

Read each line. Circle the word that is not related to the others and write its English meaning.

1. מַלְכוּתְךָ מֶלֶךְ גַּדְּלוּ יִמְלֹךְ מַלְכָּה _____

2. בִּקְדֻשָׁתוֹ קְדַשְׁתָּ קִדְּשָׁנוּ שְׁמוֹ קָדוֹשׁ _____

3. וְאָהַבְתָּ אַהֲבַת אֶחָד אַהֲבָה אוֹהֵב _____

Complete the prayer below using the three words you circled. You will need to use two of the words twice.

שְׁמַע יִשְׂרָאֵל, יְיָ אֱלֹהֵינוּ, יְיָ _____.

_____ אֱלֹהֵינוּ, גָּדוֹל אֲדוֹנֵנוּ, קָדוֹשׁ _____.

_____ לַיָי אִתִּי, וּנְרוֹמְמָה _____ יַחְדָּו.

21

Have you ever held a Torah scroll? If so, you know how heavy it is! When you celebrate your bat or bar mitzvah, just before the Torah reading begins, you (or perhaps one of your family members) are likely to have the honor of carrying the Torah, fully dressed in its mantle and ornaments, up and down the rows of congregants.

Everyone will turn to keep the Torah—and you!—in sight. Some people touch the Torah with the fringes of their **טַלִּיתוֹת** or with their **סִדּוּרִים**, which they then kiss. During the procession we sing **לְךָ יְיָ**, a prayer that praises God. It reminds us that although we *honor* the Torah, we *worship* God.

Describe how you think it will feel to carry the Torah scroll through the sanctuary.

_____

_____

Practice reading **לְךָ יְיָ**.

1. לְךָ יְיָ הַגְּדֻלָּה וְהַגְּבוּרָה וְהַתִּפְאֶרֶת וְהַנֵּצַח וְהַהוֹד,
2. כִּי כֹל בַּשָּׁמַיִם וּבָאָרֶץ, לְךָ יְיָ הַמַּמְלָכָה
3. וְהַמִּתְנַשֵּׂא לְכֹל לְרֹאשׁ.

1. *Yours, God, is the greatness, and the power, and the glory, and the eternity, and the majesty,*
2. *for all that is in heaven and on earth is Yours. Yours is the sovereignty, God,*
3. *You are supreme over all.*

Prayer Words

Practice reading these words from לְךָ יְיָ.

English	Hebrew
the greatness	הַגְּדֻלָּה
and the power	וְהַגְּבוּרָה
in heaven	בַּשָּׁמַיִם
and on earth	וּבָאָרֶץ

Search and Circle

Write the Hebrew word for each English word below. Find and circle the Hebrew words hidden in the word search grid. Look from right to left and top to bottom.

in heaven   and the power   and on earth   the greatness

_____   _____   _____   _____

ה	ב	ג	ו	א	מ	ב
ל	שׁ	ר	ה	ב	ה	י
ר	מ	ה	ג	ד	ל	ה
ג	י	ם	ב	ג	ץ	מ
ב	ם	ל	ו	י	ר	א
ו	ב	א	ר	ץ	ה	ו
ץ	ה	ר	ה	ל	ם	ג

 **Language Link**

The לְךָ יְיָ prayer teaches that everything that is in heaven (the sky) and on earth
—בַּשָּׁמַיִם וּבָאָרֶץ—is God's, for God is the Creator of the world. Here are some
examples of what is בַּשָּׁמַיִם וּבָאָרֶץ.

יָרֵחַ

פְּרָחִים

עֵצִים

שֶׁמֶשׁ

כּוֹכָבִים

הָרִים

Draw a line from each Hebrew word above to where it can be found below—in
the שָׁמַיִם or on the אֶרֶץ.

שָׁמַיִם

אֶרֶץ

You're an Artist!

Choose four or more of the
Hebrew words above and draw
a picture of yourself in nature.

Label each object you draw.
Label yourself with your Hebrew
or English name.

Partners in Prayer

Practice reading the following prayer words. Circle the two words in each line that have the same root letters. Write the root for those two words.

___ ___ ___	בַּשָּׁמַיִם	גַּדְלוּ	וּבָאָרֶץ	1. הַגְּדֻלָה
___ ___ ___	עֹז	אֶחָד	בִּקְדֻשָׁתוֹ	2. קָדוֹשׁ
___ ___ ___	וְנִשָּׂא	מֶלֶךְ	אֵין	3. מַלְכוּתְךָ
___ ___ ___	וְהַגְּבוּרָה	לְעַמּוֹ	גִּבּוֹר	4. שְׁמוֹ

Look carefully at the string of words below.

Find and circle the words that are part of כִּי מִצִיּוֹן.

אֶחָדכִּיאֱלֹהֵינוּמִצִיּוֹןגְּדוֹלְתֵצֵאאֲדוֹנֵנוּתוֹרָהַקָּדוֹשׁוּדְבַרייְשָׁמוֹמִירוּשָׁלָיִם

One of the words you did *not* circle is a Hebrew number. Write it here. _____

Use this clue to score bonus points in the "Carnival Duck!" game in Level 2 on your computer.

"Yikes!" Ben cried as he and Batya entered the tallest of Tel Aviv's three Azrieli Center towers. "It's 614 feet high with 49 floors and an observation deck. I'll ask someone where the elevator, the מַעֲלִית, is and we'll zip up. It's sure to be a high-speed מַעֲלִית because Tel Aviv is one of the most high-tech cities in the world." ▬

Torah Travel Tel Aviv has two parts: one ancient, one modern. The modern part is called Tel Aviv; the ancient part is Jaffa. That is why the city's official name is Tel Aviv-Jaffa. The Bible teaches that the prophet Jonah went to Jaffa:

יוֹנָה ... וַיֵּרֶד יָפוֹ וַיִּמְצָא אֳנִיָּה בָּאָה תַרְשִׁישׁ

"Jonah...went down to Jaffa and found a ship going to Tarshish." (Jonah 1:3).

Locate and circle Tel Aviv-Jaffa on the map on page 3.

What is the name of the highest place on which you have ever stood? How did you get to the top? What could you see? _____

_____

During the Torah service, after removing the scroll's mantle and ornaments, we open the סֵפֶר תּוֹרָה to the weekly פָּרָשָׁה. Each פָּרָשָׁה is divided into sections, or readings. For each section, one or more congregants come up to the Torah to recite two blessings—one before the Torah reader chants the section and one afterward. You will learn about both בְּרָכוֹת in this chapter.

The honor one receives when called up to recite the Torah blessings is known as an עֲלִיָּה—literally, "going up."

How do you think you will feel when you are called up for your first עֲלִיָּה as a bar or bat mitzvah?

Blessing Before the Torah Reading

We recite a blessing right before the Torah reader—בַּעַל קְרִיאָה (masculine) or בַּעֲלַת קְרִיאָה (feminine)—reads or chants each section of the פָּרָשָׁה. It is a call for the congregation to praise and thank God for giving us the Torah. The first two lines of the prayer are the same words we recite at the start of most prayer services—the בָּרְכוּ.

The person who has the honor of an aliyah—the עוֹלֶה (for a man) or עוֹלָה (for a woman)—recites the first line. The congregation responds by reciting the second line, which the עוֹלֶה or עוֹלָה then repeats before completing the prayer.

Practice reading the blessing that is recited before each section of the Torah reading.

1. בָּרְכוּ אֶת יְיָ הַמְבֹרָךְ.

2. בָּרוּךְ יְיָ הַמְבֹרָךְ לְעוֹלָם וָעֶד.

3. בָּרוּךְ אַתָּה, יְיָ אֱלֹהֵינוּ, מֶלֶךְ הָעוֹלָם,

4. אֲשֶׁר בָּחַר בָּנוּ מִכָּל הָעַמִּים,

5. וְנָתַן לָנוּ אֶת תּוֹרָתוֹ.

6. בָּרוּךְ אַתָּה, יְיָ, נוֹתֵן הַתּוֹרָה.

1. Praise Adonai, who is praised.
2. Praised is Adonai, who is praised forever and ever.
3. Praised are You, Adonai our God, Ruler of the world,
4. for choosing us from all the nations,
5. and giving us God's Torah.
6. Praised are You, Adonai, who gives us the Torah.

Prayer Words

Practice reading these words from the blessing before the Torah reading.

chose (choosing)	בָּחַר
us	בָּנוּ
from all	מִכָּל
the nations	הָעַמִּים
and gave (and giving)	וְנָתַן
to us	לָנוּ
God's Torah	תּוֹרָתוֹ
gives	נוֹתֵן

Note: תּוֹרָתוֹ literally means "his Torah," but because God is neither masculine nor feminine, we translate תּוֹרָתוֹ as "God's Torah."

P R A Y E R P U Z Z L E

Complete the puzzle by writing the Hebrew word for each English word below. Do not include the vowels or any other dots.

Down

1. the nations
2. us
3. gives
5. to us

Across

2. chose (choosing)
4. from all
6. God's Torah
7. and gave (and giving)

One or Many Chosen People?

The blessing before the Torah reading thanks God for "choosing us from all the nations" (אֲשֶׁר בָּחַר בָּנוּ מִכָּל הָעַמִּים). Some traditions teach that the Jewish people were chosen to receive the Torah and to share its teachings with the other nations of the world.

Other peoples also have traditions about their relationship with God and why they were chosen to receive their own sacred texts.

Describe something about the Jewish people that is unique or special and how it helps us add goodness to the world.

_____

_____

Describe something about yourself that is unique or special and how it helps you contribute goodness to the world.

_____

_____

Choice Voices

These phrases from the Bible express that God chose us from among the nations. Read the biblical quotes. Circle the Hebrew word for **chose** each time it appears.

1. בְּךָ בָּחַר יְיָ אֱלֹהֶיךָ לִהְיוֹת לוֹ לְעַם סְגֻלָּה

2. הָעָם בָּחַר לְנַחֲלָה לוֹ

3. כִּי־יַעֲקֹב בָּחַר לוֹ יָהּ יִשְׂרָאֵל לִסְגֻלָּתוֹ

4. וּבָחַר עוֹד בִּיְרוּשָׁלָיִם

Putting It in ConTEXT

The Hebrew words in a Torah scroll and in a printed book of the Torah are the same, but the words *look* different. The words of a Torah scroll are written without vowels and without punctuation. Every letter is handwritten by a scribe—סוֹפֵר—in calligraphy. Nine of the letters are decorated with crowns that are drawn as three vertical lines on top of the letter:

Like a scribe, draw the nine crowned letters in the numbered spaces.

א ב ג ד ה ו ה ז ח ט י כ ך ל מ ם נ ן ס ע פ ף צ ץ ק ר ש ת

—— .9 —— .8 —— .7 —— .6 —— .5 —— .4 —— .3 —— .2 —— .1

Practice reading these words from Deuteronomy.

כִּי עַם קָדוֹשׁ אַתָּה לַיהוָה אֱלֹהֶיךָ וּבְךָ בָּחַר יְהוָה...

You are a holy people to Adonai your God, for Adonai chose you... (Deuteronomy 14:2)

Now try to read the same words as they appear in the Torah scroll—סֵפֶר תּוֹרָה.

כי עם קדוש אתה ליהוה אלהיך ובך בזר יהוה

Turn to page 5 and circle the verse below as it appears in the אֵין כָּמוֹךָ blessing.
(*Remember:* יְיָ *can be written* יְהוָה.) Then read the verse as it is written below.

Adonai will rule forever and ever (Exodus 15:18) יהוה ימלך לעלם ועד

Help Is on the Way

When Torah readers prepare to read from the Torah, they often practice in a תִּקוּן a book in which the Torah text appears twice—in two different columns—on each page. In the right-hand column the text is set in regular Hebrew print with vowels, punctuation, and musical notations, or trope marks; in the left-hand column, the text looks just like it does on a Torah scroll.

דברים ואתחנן ו

וּמִצְוֹתָיו֙ אֲשֶׁ֣ר אָנֹכִ֣י מְצַוְּךָ֔ אַתָּ֖ה וּבִנְךָ֑

3 וּבֶן־בִּנְךָ֗ כֹּ֚ל יְמֵ֣י חַיֶּ֔יךָ וּלְמַ֖עַן יַאֲרִכֻ֣ן יָמֶֽיךָ׃ וְשָׁמַעְתָּ֤ יִשְׂרָאֵל֙ וְשָׁמַרְתָּ֣ לַעֲשׂ֔וֹת אֲשֶׁ֙ר יִיטַ֣ב לְךָ֔ וַאֲשֶׁ֥ר תִּרְבּ֖וּן מְאֹ֑ד כַּאֲשֶׁר֩ דִּבֶּ֙ר יְהֹוָ֜ה אֱלֹהֵ֤י אֲבֹתֶ֙יךָ֙ לָ֔ךְ אֶ֛רֶץ זָבַ֥ת חָלָ֖ב וּדְבָֽשׁ׃ פ שׁשׁי

4 שְׁמַ֖ע יִשְׂרָאֵ֑ל יְהֹוָ֥ה אֱלֹהֵ֖ינוּ יְהֹוָ֥ה ׀ אֶחָֽד׃ וְאָהַבְתָּ֔ אֵ֖ת יְהֹוָ֣ה אֱלֹהֶ֑יךָ בְּכָל־לְבָבְךָ֥ וּבְכָל־נַפְשְׁךָ֖ וּבְכָל־מְאֹדֶֽךָ׃

6 וְהָי֞וּ הַדְּבָרִ֣ים הָאֵ֗לֶּה אֲשֶׁ֙ר אָנֹכִ֧י מְצַוְּךָ֛ הַיּ֖וֹם עַל־לְבָבֶֽךָ׃

7 וְשִׁנַּנְתָּ֣ם לְבָנֶ֔יךָ וְדִבַּרְתָּ֖ בָּ֑ם בְּשִׁבְתְּךָ֤ בְּבֵיתֶ֙ךָ֙ וּבְלֶכְתְּךָ֣

8 בַדֶּ֔רֶךְ וּֽבְשָׁכְבְּךָ֖ וּבְקוּמֶֽךָ׃ וּקְשַׁרְתָּ֥ם לְא֖וֹת עַל־יָדֶ֑ךָ וְהָי֥וּ

9 לְטֹטָפֹ֖ת בֵּ֥ין עֵינֶֽיךָ׃ וּכְתַבְתָּ֛ם עַל־מְזֻז֥וֹת בֵּיתֶ֖ךָ וּבִשְׁעָרֶֽיךָ׃

10 וְהָיָ֞ה כִּ֥י יְבִיאֲךָ֣ ׀ יְהֹוָ֣ה אֱלֹהֶ֗יךָ אֶל־הָאָ֜רֶץ אֲשֶׁ֙ר נִשְׁבַּ֤ע לַאֲבֹתֶ֙יךָ֙ לְאַבְרָהָ֤ם לְיִצְחָק֙ וּֽלְיַעֲקֹ֔ב לָ֣תֶת לָ֑ךְ עָרִ֛ים

11 גְּדֹלֹ֥ת וְטֹבֹ֖ת אֲשֶׁ֥ר לֹא־בָנִֽיתָ׃ וּבָ֨תִּ֜ים מְלֵאִ֣ים כָּל־טוּב֮ אֲשֶׁ֣ר לֹא־מִלֵּאתָ֒ וּבֹרֹ֤ת חֲצוּבִים֙ אֲשֶׁ֣ר לֹא־חָצַ֔בְתָּ כְּרָמִ֥ים

12 וְזֵיתִ֖ים אֲשֶׁ֣ר לֹא־נָטָ֑עְתָּ וְאָכַלְתָּ֖ וְשָׂבָֽעְתָּ׃ הִשָּׁ֣מֶר לְךָ֔ פֶּן־תִּשְׁכַּ֖ח אֶת־יְהֹוָ֑ה אֲשֶׁ֧ר הוֹצִיאֲךָ֛ מֵאֶ֥רֶץ מִצְרַ֖יִם מִבֵּ֥ית

13 עֲבָדִֽים׃ אֶת־יְהֹוָ֧ה אֱלֹהֶ֛יךָ תִּירָ֖א וְאֹת֣וֹ תַעֲבֹ֑ד וּבִשְׁמ֖וֹ

14 תִּשָּׁבֵֽעַ׃ ס לֹ֣א תֵֽלְכ֔וּן אַחֲרֵ֖י אֱלֹהִ֣ים אֲחֵרִ֑ים מֵאֱלֹהֵי֙ הָֽעַמִּ֔ים

15 אֲשֶׁ֖ר סְבִיבֹֽתֵיכֶֽם׃ כִּ֣י אֵ֥ל קַנָּ֛א יְהֹוָ֥ה אֱלֹהֶ֖יךָ בְּקִרְבֶּ֑ךָ פֶּן־יֶ֠חֱרֶה אַף־יְהֹוָ֤ה אֱלֹהֶ֙יךָ֙ בָּ֔ךְ וְהִשְׁמִֽידְךָ֔ מֵעַ֖ל פְּנֵ֥י

16 הָאֲדָמָֽה׃ ס לֹ֣א תְנַסּ֔וּ אֶת־יְהֹוָ֖ה אֱלֹהֵיכֶ֑ם כַּאֲשֶׁ֥ר

17 נִסִּיתֶ֖ם בַּמַּסָּֽה׃ שָׁמ֣וֹר תִּשְׁמְר֔וּן אֶת־מִצְוֺ֖ת יְהֹוָ֣ה אֱלֹהֵיכֶ֑ם

וּמִצְוֹתָיו אֲשֶׁר אָנֹכִי מְצַוְּךָ אַתָּה וּבִנְךָ וּבֶן בִּנְךָ כֹּל יְמֵי חַיֶּיךָ וּלְמַעַן יַאֲרִכֻן יָמֶיךָ וְשָׁמַעְתָּ יִשְׂרָאֵל וְשָׁמַרְתָּ לַעֲשׂוֹת אֲשֶׁר יִיטַב לְךָ וַאֲשֶׁר תִּרְבּוּן מְאֹד כַּאֲשֶׁר דִּבֶּר יְהוֹה אֱלֹהֵי אֲבֹתֶיךָ לָךְ אֶרֶץ זָבַת חָלָב וּדְבָשׁ שְׁמַע יִשְׂרָאֵל יְהוֹה אֱלֹהֵינוּ יְהוֹה אֶחָד וְאָהַבְתָּ אֵת יְהוֹה אֱלֹהֶיךָ בְּכָל לְבָבְךָ וּבְכָל נַפְשְׁךָ וּבְכָל מְאֹדֶךָ וְהָיוּ הַדְּבָרִים הָאֵלֶּה אֲשֶׁר אָנֹכִי מְצַוְּךָ הַיּוֹם עַל לְבָבֶךָ וְשִׁנַּנְתָּם לְבָנֶיךָ וְדִבַּרְתָּ בָּם בְּשִׁבְתְּךָ בְּבֵיתֶךָ וּבְלֶכְתְּךָ בַדֶּרֶךְ וּבְשָׁכְבְּךָ וּבְקוּמֶךָ וּקְשַׁרְתָּם לְאוֹת עַל יָדֶךָ וְהָיוּ לְטֹטָפֹת בֵּין עֵינֶיךָ וּכְתַבְתָּם עַל מְזֻזוֹת בֵּיתֶךָ וּבִשְׁעָרֶיךָ וְהָיָה כִּי יְבִיאֲךָ יְהוֹה אֱלֹהֶיךָ אֶל הָאָרֶץ אֲשֶׁר נִשְׁבַּע לַאֲבֹתֶיךָ לְאַבְרָהָם לְיִצְחָק וּלְיַעֲקֹב לָתֶת לָךְ עָרִים גְּדֹלֹת וְטֹבֹת אֲשֶׁר לֹא בָנִיתָ וּבָתִּים מְלֵאִים כָּל טוּב אֲשֶׁר לֹא חֲצוּבִים אֲשֶׁר לֹא חָצַבְתָּ כְּרָמִים וְזֵיתִים אֲשֶׁר לֹא נָטָעְתָּ וְאָכַלְתָּ וְשָׂבָעְתָּ וְשָׁבַעְתָּ הִשָּׁמֶר לְךָ פֶּן תִּשְׁכַּח אֶת יְהוֹה אֲשֶׁר הוֹצִיאֲךָ מֵאֶרֶץ מִצְרַיִם מִבֵּית עֲבָדִים אֶת יְהוֹה אֱלֹהֶיךָ תִּירָא וְאֹתוֹ תַעֲבֹד וּבִשְׁמוֹ תִּשָּׁבֵעַ לֹא תֵלְכוּן אַחֲרֵי אֱלֹהִים אֲחֵרִים מֵאֱלֹהֵי הָעַמִּים אֲשֶׁר סְבִיבֹתֵיכֶם כִּי אֵל קַנָּא יְהוֹה אֱלֹהֶיךָ בְּקִרְבֶּךָ פֶּן יֶחֱרֶה אַף יְהוֹה אֱלֹהֶיךָ בָּךְ וְהִשְׁמִידְךָ מֵעַל פְּנֵי

Torah, Torah

Underline the six words of the שְׁמַע in each column in the תִּקוּן.

How are the two columns similar?

_____

How are they different?

_____

Bonus Points: Which prayer appears immediately after the שְׁמַע?

_____

⬯ Language Link

When someone moves from a country outside of Israel to live in יִשְׂרָאֵל, we say
he or she is making עֲלִיָּה, meaning that the person is **going up** to the holy land
of יִשְׂרָאֵל. Like a person who receives an עֲלִיָּה to the Torah, an **immigrant** is
called an עוֹלֶה (masculine) or עוֹלָה (feminine).

These Hebrew words—עֲלִיָּה, עוֹלֶה, and עוֹלָה—are all built on the root עלה.
Words that are built on the root עלה have **going up** as part of their meaning.

Why do you think Jewish tradition teaches that, like having an עֲלִיָּה, immigrating
to Israel brings us to a higher spiritual level? _____

_____

The following two words are also built on the root עלה.

elevator   מַעֲלִית   degree (of heat or cold)   מַעֲלָה

What do a מַעֲלִית and a מַעֲלָה have in common? _____

Draw a line from the words that are built on the root עלה to the jet.

מַעֲלִית   עוֹלָה   יִשְׂרָאֵל   מַעֲלָה   תּוֹרָתוֹ   עֲלִיָּה

Blessing After the Torah Reading

The blessing after each section of the פָּרָשָׁה praises God for giving us the Torah of truth and for the eternal life the Torah gives us.

Why do you think we call the Torah "Torah of truth"?

_____

_____

How does rereading the Torah, year after year, and passing its lessons on from one generation to the next, help give the Jewish people "eternal life"?

_____

_____

Practice reading the blessing after the Torah reading.

1. בָּרוּךְ אַתָּה, יְיָ אֱלֹהֵינוּ, מֶלֶךְ הָעוֹלָם,

2. אֲשֶׁר נָתַן לָנוּ תּוֹרַת אֱמֶת,

3. וְחַיֵּי עוֹלָם נָטַע בְּתוֹכֵנוּ.

4. בָּרוּךְ אַתָּה, יְיָ, נוֹתֵן הַתּוֹרָה.

1. *Praised are You, Adonai our God, Ruler of the world,*
2. *who gave us the Torah of truth,*
3. *and planted eternal life in us.*
4. *Praised are You, Adonai, who gives us the Torah.*

Congratulations!

It is a custom to congratulate people who have just had an עֲלִיָּה or other Torah honor. One popular expression of congratulations is יִישַׁר כֹּחַ ("Strength to you"). Another is חֲזַק וּבָרוּךְ ("Be strong and be blessed").

Prayer Words

Practice reading these words from the blessing.

Torah of	תּוֹרַת
truth	אֱמֶת
and life (of)	וְחַיֵּי
eternal, world	עוֹלָם

High-Tech Israel

Write the Hebrew word for each English meaning.

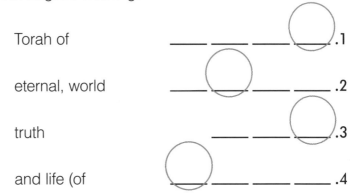

Torah of	_____ _____ _____⃝ .1
eternal, world	_____ ⃝_____ _____ .2
truth	_____ _____⃝ .3
and life (of	⃝_____ _____ _____ .4

Copy the letters from the circles to the lines below to complete the name of the most high-tech city in Israel.

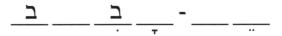

ב ___ ב ___ - ___ ___

Now draw a line from each prayer word in the top row to a related word from the siddur in the bottom row.

עוֹלָם	וְחַיֵּי	אֱמֶת	תּוֹרַת
בְּתוֹרָתֶךָ	בֶּאֱמֶת	הָעוֹלָמִים	לְחַיִּים

וְזֹאת הַתּוֹרָה

After we finish reading from the סֵפֶר תּוֹרָה (Torah scroll), an honoree comes to the בִּימָה, grasps the scroll by its wooden rollers, and raises it high. Looking at the open scroll, the congregation proudly sings וְזֹאת הַתּוֹרָה declaring that the words we read at the Torah service are the very same ones that Moses shared with the Israelites in the wilderness of Sinai almost 3,500 years ago.

The ritual of raising the Torah for the congregation to see is called הַגְבָּהָה. The person who raises the Torah is called מַגְבִּיהַ (masculine) or מַגְבִּיהָה (feminine).

Why is it important that the Torah's words have remained the same for thousands of years, so that generations of Jews hear and study the same text?

_____

_____

Do you think that each generation of the Jewish people finds the same meaning in the words of the Torah, or different meanings? Explain your answer.

_____

_____

Practice reading וְזֹאת הַתּוֹרָה.

1. וְזֹאת הַתּוֹרָה אֲשֶׁר שָׂם מֹשֶׁה לִפְנֵי בְּנֵי יִשְׂרָאֵל,

2. עַל־פִּי יְיָ בְּיַד מֹשֶׁה.

1. This is the Torah that Moses set before the people of Israel,
2. the word of Adonai by the hand of Moses.

וְזֹאת הַתּוֹרָה

Prayer Words

Practice reading these words from וְזֹאת הַתּוֹרָה.

and this is	וְזֹאת
that, which	אֲשֶׁר
set, put	שָׂם
Moses	מֹשֶׁה
before	לִפְנֵי
by the hand of	בְּיַד

Picture That!

Draw a line to connect each Hebrew phrase to its English meaning.
Hint: If you need help, turn to page 35.

that Moses set	לִפְנֵי בְּנֵי יִשְׂרָאֵל
and this is the Torah	בְּיַד מֹשֶׁה
by the hand of Moses	אֲשֶׁר שָׂם מֹשֶׁה
before the people of Israel	וְזֹאת הַתּוֹרָה

Circle the Hebrew word that appears in two of these phrases.

Now choose one of the above phrases and draw a picture to illustrate it. Write the phrase in Hebrew next to the illustration.

Putting It in ConTEXT

The words of the prayer וְזֹאת הַתּוֹרָה are taken from the Torah. Below are two verses from the Torah. Underline all the words that also appear in וְזֹאת הַתּוֹרָה. (Remember: יְיָ can be written יְהֹוָה.) Practice reading all the lines aloud.

1. וְזֹאת הַתּוֹרָה אֲשֶׁר שָׂם מֹשֶׁה לִפְנֵי בְּנֵי יִשְׂרָאֵל.

2. עַל־פִּי יְהֹוָה יַחֲנוּ וְעַל־פִּי יְהֹוָה יִסָּעוּ אֶת־מִשְׁמֶרֶת יְהֹוָה שָׁמָרוּ עַל־פִּי יְהֹוָה בְּיַד מֹשֶׁה.

Dressing the Torah

After raising the Torah for the congregation to see (הַגְבָּהָה), we roll it closed, bind it, and dress it in its cover and ornaments. The honor of rolling and dressing the Torah is called גְּלִילָה. The person who is honored is called גּוֹלֵל (masculine) or גּוֹלֶלֶת (feminine).

Use the following words to complete the prayer phrases. Circle the word that you use twice.

תּוֹרָתוֹ   תּוֹרַת   הַתּוֹרָה

1. אֲשֶׁר בָּחַר בָּנוּ מִכָּל הָעַמִּים, וְנָתַן לָנוּ אֶת _____

2. בָּרוּךְ אַתָּה, יְיָ, נוֹתֵן _____

3. אֲשֶׁר נָתַן לָנוּ _____ אֱמֶת

4. וְזֹאת _____ אֲשֶׁר שָׂם מֹשֶׁה לִפְנֵי בְּנֵי יִשְׂרָאֵל

Which word is the name of the prophet who set the Torah before the people of Israel? _____ Place this clue in its correct spot in the "Stampede" game in Level 3 on your computer.

"Mount Carmel is *the* place for camping," Batya said to her dad as they looked out on the pine-covered mountain range. "Let's get Ben, put out our campfire and clean up our campground, and then drive on to Haifa." ▮▬

Torah Travel When the prophet Elijah wanted to inspire our ancestors to have faith in God, he told King Ahab,

וְעַתָּה שְׁלַח קְבֹץ אֵלַי אֶת־כָּל־יִשְׂרָאֵל אֶל־הַר הַכַּרְמֶל...

"Now bid all Israel to join me at Mount Carmel..." (I Kings 18:19).

Haifa, the third largest city in Israel, sits on the northern part of Mount Carmel and overlooks the Mediterranean Sea. Locate and circle Haifa—חֵיפָה—on the map of Israel on page 3.

How did Batya show she knows what's right and wrong when camping?

_____

_____

The biblical prophets were known as God's messengers—righteous people who instructed our ancestors in the Torah's lessons of right and wrong. Some say the prophets are the conscience of the Jewish people.

What do you think it means that "the prophets are the conscience of the Jewish people"?

_____

_____

On Shabbat, after completing the Torah portion, we read a selection from the Prophets. It is called a הַפְטָרָה ("conclusion"). The haftarah's teachings can deepen and enrich our understanding of the פָּרָשָׁה. Before and after chanting the הַפְטָרָה we recite blessings that praise God for giving us the prophets.

It's an Honor

The last person called to the Torah on Shabbat is called the מַפְטִיר (masculine) or מַפְטִירָה (feminine). That person is often the bar or bat mitzvah. Usually, the מַפְטִיר or מַפְטִירָה also chants the הַפְטָרָה blessings and the הַפְטָרָה itself.

Why do you think the bar or bat mitzvah is the one who chants the הַפְטָרָה?

_____

_____

Practice reading the blessing that is recited before the הַפְטָרָה.

1. בָּרוּךְ אַתָּה, יְיָ אֱלֹהֵינוּ, מֶלֶךְ הָעוֹלָם, אֲשֶׁר בָּחַר בִּנְבִיאִים טוֹבִים,

2. וְרָצָה בְדִבְרֵיהֶם הַנֶּאֱמָרִים בֶּאֱמֶת.

3. בָּרוּךְ אַתָּה, יְיָ, הַבּוֹחֵר בַּתּוֹרָה וּבְמשֶׁה עַבְדוֹ,

4. וּבְיִשְׂרָאֵל עַמּוֹ, וּבִנְבִיאֵי הָאֱמֶת וָצֶדֶק.

1. *Praised are You, Adonai our God, Ruler of the world, who chose good prophets,*
2. *and was pleased with their words spoken in truth.*
3. *Praised are You, Adonai, the One who chooses (takes delight in) the Torah, and Moses, God's servant,*
4. *and Israel, God's people, and prophets of truth and righteousness (justice).*

Three-Part Harmony

The Bible (תָּנָ"ךְ) consists of three parts: The Torah (תּוֹרָה), Prophets (נְבִיאִים), and Writings (כְּתוּבִים), which includes psalms, poems, and proverbs. There are musical notations, or trope, for the תּוֹרָה portions, הַפְטָרָה readings, and some of the books of כְּתוּבִים. The trope appears as markings under and over the words of the Hebrew text.

Prayer Words

Practice reading these words from the blessing recited before the הַפְטָרָה.

prophets	נְבִיאִים
good	טוֹבִים
with their words	בְּדִבְרֵיהֶם
spoken	הַנֶּאֱמָרִים
in truth	בֶּאֱמֶת
his (God's) servant	עַבְדּוֹ
and righteousness (justice)	וָצֶדֶק

This is a street sign in Jerusalem. Write the name of the street in English:

Street of the _____

Siddur Challenge

Write the number of each Hebrew word next to the matching English.

4. בֶּאֱמֶת   3. טוֹבִים   2. וָצֶדֶק   1. הַנֶּאֱמָרִים

7. בְּדִבְרֵיהֶם   6. עַבְדּוֹ   5. נְבִיאִים

_____ God's servant   _____ spoken   _____ with their words

_____ good   _____ prophets

Two important Hebrew words are left. Write each word on the right side below and its English meaning on the left.

_____ = _____   _____ = _____

 **At the Root**

בְּדִבְרֵיהֶם means **with their words**.

The root of בְּדִבְרֵיהֶם is דבר.

The root דבר tells us that **word** or **speak** is part of a word's meaning.

Circle the root letters דבר in the words below.

דּוֹבְרֵי   מְדַבֶּרֶת   דְּבָרִים   כִּדְבָרֶיךָ   נְדַבְּרָנוּ   דִּבֶּר

Bonus Points: Turn to the כִּי מִצִּיּוֹן prayer on page 15 and find the word built on the

root דבר. Write it here. _____

Bible Speak

1. The last book of the Torah, Deuteronomy, is called דְּבָרִים in Hebrew because דְּבָרִים is the first key word in the book. דְּבָרִים starts with these words:

אֵלֶּה הַדְּבָרִים אֲשֶׁר דִּבֶּר מֹשֶׁה אֶל־כָּל־יִשְׂרָאֵל

Circle the words that are built on the root דבר.

2. The last book of the Bible, Chronicles, is called דִּבְרֵי הַיָּמִים in Hebrew. Circle the part of the name that is built on the root דבר.

3. In synagogue, the prayer leader or the bat or bar mitzvah may speak about a lesson from the הַפְטָרָה or פָּרָשָׁה. The speech is called a דְּבַר תּוֹרָה. Circle the root letters in דְּבַר תּוֹרָה that let you know that **word** or **speak** is part of its meaning.

Language Link

Israel is a democracy. Israelis vote for their leaders in an election. The Hebrew word for **elections** is בְּחִירוֹת. The word בְּחִירוֹת is built on the root בחר. Words built on the root בחר have **choose** or **select** as part of their meaning.

Circle the words in the הַפְטָרָה blessing on page 39 that are also built on the root בחר.

Imagine that your class was planning a trip to Israel and had to choose where the class would go first. Circle your choice below and explain why.

Jerusalem / יְרוּשָׁלַיִם   Tel Aviv / תֵּל־אָבִיב   Negev / נֶגֶב   Haifa / חֵיפָה

_____

_____

Just for Fun: A Hebrew word that may be used on election day is קַנְדִידָט (masculine) / קַנְדִידָטָה (feminine). What do you think it means in English?

_____

 ## Reader's Choice

Read these lines from the Prophets—נְבִיאִים.

1. וְאִם רַע בְּעֵינֵיכֶם לַעֲבֹד אֶת־יְהוָֹה בַּחֲרוּ לָכֶם הַיּוֹם אֶת־מִי תַעֲבֹדוּן...

2. וַיִּקַּח מַקְלוֹ בְּיָדוֹ וַיִּבְחַר־לוֹ חֲמִשָּׁה חַלֻּקֵי אֲבָנִים...

3. וְיִתְּנוּ־לָנוּ שְׁנַיִם פָּרִים וְיִבְחֲרוּ לָהֶם הַפָּר הָאֶחָד...

In each line, circle the word that is built on the root בחר.

The circled words have _____ or _____ as part of their meaning.

Blessings After the Haftarah Is Chanted

Several blessings are recited after the haftarah reading. This book gives two versions of these blessings. One is on this page; it is recited in Reform synagogues. The other is on pages 44–45; it is recited in Conservative synagogues. Both versions express gratitude for God's faithfulness, compassion, and steadfastness.

Think of what it means for a *person* to be "faithful, compassionate, and steadfast." Which attribute do you consider most important? Why?

_____

_____

Blessings recited after the haftarah in Reform synagogues

1. בָּרוּךְ אַתָּה, יְיָ אֱלֹהֵינוּ, מֶלֶךְ הָעוֹלָם, צוּר כָּל הָעוֹלָמִים,

2. צַדִּיק בְּכָל הַדּוֹרוֹת, הָאֵל הַנֶּאֱמָן, הָאוֹמֵר וְעֹשֶׂה,

3. הַמְדַבֵּר וּמְקַיֵּם, שֶׁכָּל דְּבָרָיו אֱמֶת וָצֶדֶק.

4. עַל הַתּוֹרָה, וְעַל הָעֲבוֹדָה, וְעַל הַנְּבִיאִים, וְעַל יוֹם הַשַּׁבָּת הַזֶּה,

5. שֶׁנָּתַתָּ לָּנוּ יְיָ אֱלֹהֵינוּ, לִקְדֻשָּׁה וְלִמְנוּחָה, לְכָבוֹד וּלְתִפְאָרֶת.

6. עַל הַכֹּל יְיָ אֱלֹהֵינוּ, אֲנַחְנוּ מוֹדִים לָךְ, וּמְבָרְכִים אוֹתָךְ.

7. יִתְבָּרַךְ שִׁמְךָ בְּפִי כָּל חַי תָּמִיד לְעוֹלָם וָעֶד.

8. בָּרוּךְ אַתָּה, יְיָ, מְקַדֵּשׁ הַשַּׁבָּת.

1. *Praised are You, Adonai our God, Ruler of the world, Rock of all eternity,*
2. *righteous in all generations, the faithful God, the One who says and does,*
3. *the One who speaks and fulfills, for all God's words are truthful and just.*
4. *For the Torah, for worship, for the prophets, and for this Shabbat day,*
5. *that You have given to us, Adonai our God, for holiness and for rest, for honor and for glory.*
6. *For all of this, Adonai our God, we thank You, and praise You.*
7. *May Your name be praised forever by every living being.*
8. *Praised are You, Adonai, who makes Shabbat holy.*

Blessings recited after the haftarah in Conservative synagogues

1. בָּרוּךְ אַתָּה, יְיָ אֱלֹהֵינוּ, מֶלֶךְ הָעוֹלָם, צוּר כָּל הָעוֹלָמִים,

2. צַדִּיק בְּכָל הַדּוֹרוֹת, הָאֵל הַנֶּאֱמָן, הָאוֹמֵר וְעֹשֶׂה,

3. הַמְדַבֵּר וּמְקַיֵּם, שֶׁכָּל דְּבָרָיו אֱמֶת וָצֶדֶק.

4. נֶאֱמָן אַתָּה הוּא יְיָ אֱלֹהֵינוּ, וְנֶאֱמָנִים דְּבָרֶיךָ,

5. וְדָבָר אֶחָד מִדְּבָרֶיךָ אָחוֹר לֹא יָשׁוּב רֵיקָם,

6. כִּי אֵל מֶלֶךְ נֶאֱמָן וְרַחֲמָן אָתָּה.

7. בָּרוּךְ אַתָּה, יְיָ, הָאֵל הַנֶּאֱמָן בְּכָל דְּבָרָיו.

8. רַחֵם עַל צִיּוֹן כִּי הִיא בֵּית חַיֵּינוּ, וְלַעֲלוּבַת נֶפֶשׁ תּוֹשִׁיעַ

9. בִּמְהֵרָה בְיָמֵינוּ. בָּרוּךְ אַתָּה יְיָ, מְשַׂמֵּחַ צִיּוֹן בְּבָנֶיהָ.

1. Praised are You, Adonai our God, Ruler of the world, Rock of all eternity,
2. righteous in all generations, the faithful God, the One who says and does,
3. the One who speaks and fulfills, for all God's words are truthful and just.
4. You are faithful, Adonai our God, and faithful are Your words,
5. and not one of Your words will return empty,
6. for You are a faithful and compassionate God and Ruler.
7. Praised are You, Adonai, faithful in all Your words
8. Have mercy on Zion, the source of our life; bring hope to the humbled spirit,
9. speedily in our time. Praised are You, Adonai, who gladdens Zion through her children.

צֶדֶק

10. שַׂמְּחֵנוּ, יְיָ אֱלֹהֵינוּ, בְּאֵלִיָּהוּ הַנָּבִיא עַבְדֶּךָ, וּבְמַלְכוּת בֵּית דָּוִד מְשִׁיחֶךָ,

11. בִּמְהֵרָה יָבֹא וְיָגֵל לִבֵּנוּ, עַל כִּסְאוֹ לֹא יֵשֵׁב זָר,

12. וְלֹא יִנְחֲלוּ עוֹד אֲחֵרִים אֶת כְּבוֹדוֹ, כִּי בְּשֵׁם קָדְשְׁךָ נִשְׁבַּעְתָּ

13. לוֹ שֶׁלֹּא יִכְבֶּה נֵרוֹ לְעוֹלָם וָעֶד. בָּרוּךְ אַתָּה, יְיָ, מָגֵן דָּוִד.

14. עַל הַתּוֹרָה, וְעַל הָעֲבוֹדָה, וְעַל הַנְּבִיאִים, וְעַל יוֹם הַשַּׁבָּת הַזֶּה,

15. שֶׁנָּתַתָּ לָנוּ יְיָ אֱלֹהֵינוּ, לִקְדֻשָּׁה וְלִמְנוּחָה, לְכָבוֹד וּלְתִפְאָרֶת.

16. עַל הַכֹּל יְיָ אֱלֹהֵינוּ, אֲנַחְנוּ מוֹדִים לָךְ, וּמְבָרְכִים אוֹתָךְ.

17. יִתְבָּרַךְ שִׁמְךָ בְּפִי כָּל חַי תָּמִיד לְעוֹלָם וָעֶד.

18. בָּרוּךְ אַתָּה, יְיָ, מְקַדֵּשׁ הַשַּׁבָּת.

10. *Bring joy to us, Adonai our God, through Your servant Elijah the prophet, and the kingdom of the house of David, Your anointed one.*

11. *May he (Elijah) come speedily and gladden our hearts. May no stranger sit on his (David's) throne*

12. *nor permit others to inherit his honor, for by Your holy name, You promised*

13. *him that his light would not be extinguished forever and ever. Praised are You, Adonai, Shield of David.*

14. *For the Torah, and for worship, and for the prophets, and for this Shabbat day,*

15. *that You have given to us, Adonai our God, for holiness and for rest, for honor and for glory.*

16. *For all of this, Adonai our God, we thank You, and praise You.*

17. *May Your name be praised forever by every living being.*

18. *Praised are You, Adonai, who makes Shabbat holy.*

Prayer Words

Practice reading these words from the blessings that are recited after the הַפְטָרָה.

rock	צוּר
the One who is faithful	הַנֶּאֱמָן
the One who says	הָאוֹמֵר
for honor	לִכְבוֹד
thank (plural)	מוֹדִים
forever	תָּמִיד

Finish the Phrases

Complete each prayer phrase with the missing Hebrew word. *Hint:* If you need help, turn to page 43 or to pages 44–45.

1. וְעֹשֶׂה _____
2. אֲנַחְנוּ _____ לָךְ
3. כָּל הָעוֹלָמִים _____
4. וּלְתִפְאָרֶת _____
5. בְּפִי כָל חַי _____ לְעוֹלָם וָעֶד
6. הָאֵל _____

Challenge: Draw a picture of the word you wrote in #3 above.

46

 **At the Root**

The root of הָאוֹמֵר is אמר.

The root אמר tells us that **say** is part of a word's meaning.

Circle the three root letters in הָאוֹמֵר.

What might the prayer mean when it calls God הָאוֹמֵר "the One who says"? In what ways might God "speak"? _____

_____

Putting It in ConTEXT

The closing blessings of the haftarah describe God as "the One who says and does." In the text below, the prophet Isaiah says on behalf of God:

הָעֲנִיִּים וְהָאֶבְיוֹנִים מְבַקְשִׁים מַיִם וָאַיִן לְשׁוֹנָם בַּצָּמָא
נָשָׁתָּה אֲנִי יְהֹוָה אֶעֱנֵם אֱלֹהֵי יִשְׂרָאֵל לֹא אֶעֶזְבֵם.

The poor and the needy seek water, and there is none. Their tongue is parched with thirst. I, Adonai, will respond to them. I, the God of Israel, will not forsake them. (Isaiah 41:17)

What role can people play in turning God's promises into reality?

_____

_____

צוּר

Returning the Torah Scroll to the Ark

Before putting the Torah back in the Ark, the congregation stands and the prayer leader recites the יְהַלְלוּ prayer, which praises God.

יְהַלְלוּ אֶת שֵׁם יְיָ, כִּי נִשְׂגָּב שְׁמוֹ לְבַדּוֹ. ‎1.

1. Praise the Name of Adonai, for God's Name alone is exalted.

The congregation responds by reciting the הוֹדוֹ prayer, which says God praises us.

הוֹדוֹ עַל אֶרֶץ וְשָׁמָיִם. וַיָּרֶם קֶרֶן לְעַמּוֹ, ‎2.

תְּהִלָּה לְכָל־חֲסִידָיו, לִבְנֵי יִשְׂרָאֵל עַם־קְרֹבוֹ, הַלְלוּ־יָהּ! ‎3.

2. God's splendor is on heaven and earth. God has raised the horn of God's people (made them safe),

3. giving praise to all of God's faithful, to the Children of Israel, the people close to God. Halleluyah!

Line 3 says our people are "close to God." What do you think that means?

_____

_____

After reciting the הוֹדוֹ prayer, some congregations sing Psalm 29 when they return the סֵפֶר תּוֹרָה to the Ark.

סִפְרֵי תּוֹרָה

Prayer Words

Practice reading these words from the יְהַלְלוּ and הוֹדוּ prayers.

(let us) praise	יְהַלְלוּ
name	שֵׁם
praise	תְּהִלָּה

Rhyme Time

Connect each word in column א to a rhyming word in column ב. Then write the English meaning for each word in column ב.

ב		א
	יְהַלְלוּ	תְּפִלָּה
_____	תְּהִלָּה	הֵם
_____	שֵׁם	יְחַלְלוּ

Bonus Points: Write your שֵׁם in Hebrew. _____

שֵׁם

49

עֵץ חַיִּים הִיא

The Torah is often called a tree of life. Just as a tree sustains life through its fruit, oxygen, and shade, the Torah keeps us alive and strong through its teachings, such as the values of justice, peace, and rest on Shabbat. The Torah not only helps keep our bodies and spirits healthy, it also gives us a sense of purpose by telling us to improve the world.

The roots of the Torah are strong and deep, going back thousands of years to our ancestors who first received it at Mount Sinai. Its branches are forever expanding as each new generation studies the Torah and adds its understandings to our tradition.

Name another item in nature to which you might compare the Torah and explain why you made this choice.

_____

_____

_____

When the Torah scroll is placed inside the Ark, the congregation remains standing and recites the כִּי לֶקַח and עֵץ חַיִּים prayers.

כִּי לֶקַח טוֹב נָתַתִּי לָכֶם, תּוֹרָתִי אַל תַּעֲזֹבוּ.

For I have given you precious teaching; do not abandon My Torah.

1. עֵץ חַיִּים הִיא לַמַּחֲזִיקִים בָּהּ, וְתֹמְכֶיהָ מְאֻשָּׁר.

2. דְּרָכֶיהָ דַרְכֵי נֹעַם, וְכָל נְתִיבוֹתֶיהָ שָׁלוֹם.

3. הֲשִׁיבֵנוּ יְיָ אֵלֶיךָ וְנָשׁוּבָה, חַדֵּשׁ יָמֵינוּ כְּקֶדֶם.

1. *It (the Torah) is a tree of life to those who uphold it, and those who support it are happy.*
2. *Its ways are ways of pleasantness and all its paths are peace.*
3. *Bring us back to You, Adonai, and we will return; renew our days as of old.*

Prayer Words

Practice reading these words from עֵץ חַיִּים.

tree of life	עֵץ חַיִּים
happy	מְאֻשָּׁר
its ways, its paths	דְּרָכֶיהָ
pleasantness	נֹעַם
renew	חַדֵּשׁ
our days	יָמֵינוּ

Clue to Cyberspace

Read the words below. Then choose and write the Hebrew word from the list above that is similar to the words on each line.

1.	נָעִים	וּבִנְעִימָה	נְעִימוֹת	_____
2.	תִּדְרֹךְ	דְּרָכָיו	דֶּרֶךְ	_____
3.	יוֹם	יָמִים	יְמֵי	_____
4.	אַשְׁרֵי	תְּאַשֵּׁר	וְאִשְׁרוּ	_____
5.	מְחַדֵּשׁ	חָדָשׁ	וַחֲדָשָׁה	_____

Which phrase from "Prayer Words" is left? _____

Draw an illustration to represent this phrase.

Use this clue to complete the last board in the "Lion's Bird House" game in Lesson 4 on your computer.

עָלֵינוּ 5

" I 'm so glad we joined the Israeli Scouts—the **צוֹפִים**," said Ben, as he, Batya, and the other **צוֹפִים** climbed the ancient fortress of Masada in the Judean Desert. "It's cool that in the **צוֹפִים** we can learn about leadership and how to be prepared for wilderness survival."

"Yup," agreed Batya. "And that includes being prepared to be loyal and trustworthy. Remember the **צוֹפִים** oath: 'I promise to do my best to fulfill my duties to my people, my country, and my land, to help others at all times and to obey scout law.'"

In what ways do you show loyalty to your country now? _____

_____

עָלֵינוּ, one of the closing prayers of the service, is a pledge of loyalty and obligation to God. When we recite **עָלֵינוּ** we praise and worship God as the One Creator and Ruler. We declare our people's loyalty to God and our desire for peace and a better world.

✈ **Torah Travel** Even before he was king, David declared his loyalty to God.

מִזְמוֹר לְדָוִד בִּהְיוֹתוֹ בְּמִדְבַּר יְהוּדָה: אֱלֹהִים אֵלִי אַתָּה...

"A psalm of David when he was in the Judean Desert: God, You are my God...."

(Psalms 63:1)

Locate and circle Masada—**מְצָדָה**—on the map on page 3.

Why are giving **צְדָקָה**, pursuing peace and justice, and praying considered ways to show loyalty to God?

_____

_____

A Prayer of Loyalty and Defiance

עָלֵינוּ was written about 2,000 years ago. We do not know who wrote it. It was added to the Rosh Hashanah service in the third century CE and, in about the thirteenth century, it became part of the daily service.

It is a tradition to stand when reciting עָלֵינוּ. It is also a tradition to bend our knees and bow from the waist as a sign of honor and respect for God when we say line 4 below. As we begin line 5, we stand straight again.

Name two prayers in other sections of the service in which we bow.

_____   _____

Practice reading עָלֵינוּ.

1. עָלֵינוּ לְשַׁבֵּחַ לַאֲדוֹן הַכֹּל, לָתֵת גְּדֻלָּה לְיוֹצֵר בְּרֵאשִׁית,

2. שֶׁלֹּא עָשָׂנוּ כְּגוֹיֵי הָאֲרָצוֹת, וְלֹא שָׂמָנוּ כְּמִשְׁפְּחוֹת הָאֲדָמָה,

3. שֶׁלֹּא שָׂם חֶלְקֵנוּ כָּהֶם, וְגֹרָלֵנוּ כְּכָל־הֲמוֹנָם,

4. וַאֲנַחְנוּ כּוֹרְעִים וּמִשְׁתַּחֲוִים וּמוֹדִים,

5. לִפְנֵי מֶלֶךְ מַלְכֵי הַמְּלָכִים, הַקָּדוֹשׁ בָּרוּךְ הוּא.

1. *It is upon us (our duty) to praise the God of all, to praise the Creator of the universe,*
2. *who did not make us like the other nations of the world, and did not set us like the other families of the earth,*
3. *who did not appoint our lot to be like the others, and gave us a unique destiny.*
4. *We bend the knee, bow, and give thanks*
5. *before the Ruler of the rulers of rulers, the blessed Holy One.*

6. שֶׁהוּא נוֹטֶה שָׁמַיִם וְיֹסֵד אָרֶץ,

7. וּמוֹשַׁב יְקָרוֹ בַּשָּׁמַיִם מִמַּעַל וּשְׁכִינַת עֻזּוֹ בְּגָבְהֵי מְרוֹמִים.

8. הוּא אֱלֹהֵינוּ אֵין עוֹד, אֱמֶת מַלְכֵּנוּ אֶפֶס זוּלָתוֹ.

9. כַּכָּתוּב בְּתוֹרָתוֹ, וְיָדַעְתָּ הַיּוֹם וַהֲשֵׁבֹתָ אֶל לְבָבֶךָ,

10. כִּי יְיָ הוּא הָאֱלֹהִים בַּשָּׁמַיִם מִמַּעַל, וְעַל הָאָרֶץ מִתָּחַת, אֵין עוֹד.

6. God spreads out the heavens and establishes the earth,
7. God's glorious abode is in the heavens above and God's powerful Presence is in the highest of heights.
8. God is our God, there is no other. True that God is our Ruler, there is none besides God.
9. As it is written in God's Torah: Know on that day and take it to heart,
10. that Adonai is God in the heavens above, and on the earth below; there is no other.

11. וְנֶאֱמַר, וְהָיָה יְיָ לְמֶלֶךְ עַל כָּל הָאָרֶץ.

12. בַּיּוֹם הַהוּא יִהְיֶה יְיָ אֶחָד וּשְׁמוֹ אֶחָד.

11. And it is said: Adonai will rule all the land.
12. On that day, Adonai will be One and God's name will be One.

A Feeling of Belonging

Many of the words in עָלֵינוּ end with the suffix נוּ, meaning **us** or **our**. Circle all the words in עָלֵינוּ that end with נוּ. How many words did you circle? _____

Saying "us" and "our" rather than "me" and "my" reminds us that we are part of a community.

What do you think is the most important role of the synagogue community?

_____

What do you like most about being part of your synagogue community?

_____

Prayer Words

Practice reading these words from עָלֵינוּ.

it is upon us (our duty)	עָלֵינוּ
to praise	לְשַׁבֵּחַ
to God	לַאֲדוֹן
of all	הַכֹּל
and we	וַאֲנַחְנוּ
bend the knee	כּוֹרְעִים
Ruler of the rulers of rulers	מֶלֶךְ מַלְכֵי הַמְּלָכִים
and it is said	וְנֶאֱמַר

Write the Hebrew word for each English word below. Find and circle the Hebrew words hidden in the word search grid. Look from right to left and top to bottom. Then copy the letters you have *not* circled on to the lines below.

1. to God _____

2. bend the knee _____

3. and it is said _____

4. to praise _____

5. and we _____

6. it is our duty _____

7. of all _____

כ	ו	ר	ע	י	ם
ו	ה	כ	ל	ע	ו	מ
א	ל	ל	ךְ	ל	נ	מ
נ	ל	שׁ	כ	י	א	י
ח	ה	ב	מ	נ	מ	ל
נ	כ	ח	י	ו	ר	ם
ו	ל	א	ד	ו	ן

Another name for God is:

___ ___ ___ ___ ___ ___ ___

Collective Thanks

The word וּמוֹדִים tells us that עָלֵינוּ is a prayer of thanks as well as a declaration of loyalty. וּמוֹדִים means **and (we) give thanks**. The prefix וּ means **and**; the suffix יִם. tells us that the verb is in the plural form.

Do you think it is significant that "and we give thanks" is in the plural form?
Why or why not? _____

There are many other prayers of thanks. For example, each morning it is a tradition to recite a personal prayer of thanks to God, the אֲנִי מוֹדֶה/מוֹדָה.

How can it help us to start each day with words and thoughts of thanks and gratitude?

_____

In modern Hebrew, the way to say **thanks a lot** is תּוֹדָה רַבָּה. Circle the word in that phrase that is in the same word family as וּמוֹדִים, מוֹדֶה, מוֹדָה, and.

Name someone who has been kind or helpful to you. In the speech bubble, write "thanks a lot" in Hebrew.

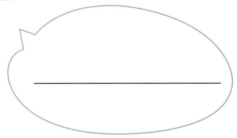

Thanksgiving in the Bible

Read these words of thanksgiving from the Bible.

In each line, find and circle the word of thanks, תּוֹדָה.

Remember: Sometimes a word includes prefixes.

1. וְקַטֵּר מֵחָמֵץ תּוֹדָה וְקִרְאוּ נְדָבוֹת הַשְׁמִיעוּ...

2. וַאֲנִי בְּקוֹל תּוֹדָה אֶזְבְּחָה-לָּךְ אֲשֶׁר נָדַרְתִּי אֲשַׁלֵּמָה...

3. וְהַתּוֹדָה הַשֵּׁנִית הַהוֹלֶכֶת לְמוֹאל וַאֲנִי אַחֲרֶיהָ...

 **Language Link**

The phrase בַּיּוֹם הַהוּא means **on that day**. In עָלֵינוּ it refers to the time when the world will be perfect. The Hebrew word for **day** is יוֹם.

Practice reading the days of the week in Hebrew.

Sunday (Day 1)	יוֹם רִאשׁוֹן
Monday (Day 2)	יוֹם שֵׁנִי
Tuesday (Day 3)	יוֹם שְׁלִישִׁי
Wednesday (Day 4)	יוֹם רְבִיעִי
Thursday (Day 5)	יוֹם חֲמִישִׁי
Friday (Day 6)	יוֹם שִׁשִׁי
Saturday (Shabbat)	יוֹם שַׁבָּת

What Bible story in the Book of Genesis do the names of the days remind you of? Why?

_____

_____

עֶרֶב שַׁבָּת means the **eve of Shabbat**, Friday night.

יוֹם שַׁבָּת means the **day of Shabbat**, Saturday.

Fill in the missing Hebrew word that tells when we light Shabbat candles.

_____ שַׁבָּת

Did you know that Sunday is a weekday in Israel? In fact, Jewish Israeli kids go to school יוֹם רִאשׁוֹן through יוֹם שִׁשִׁי. The good news is that Jewish religious holidays, like רֹאשׁ הַשָּׁנָה and פֶּסַח, are also national holidays and days off from school!

Putting It in ConTEXT

Reread line 6 of עָלֵינוּ, which describes God as the Creator of the world.

נוֹטֶה שָׁמַיִם וְיֹסֵד אָרֶץ

This line comes from the book of the prophet Isaiah (51:13). Other lines in Isaiah (42:5) also describe God as the Creator of the world.

כֹּה־אָמַר הָאֵל יְהֹוָה בּוֹרֵא הַשָּׁמַיִם וְנוֹטֵיהֶם

רֹקַע הָאָרֶץ וְצֶאֱצָאֶיהָ...

Thus says God, Adonai, who created the heavens and stretched them out,
Who spread forth the earth and all that comes out of it …

Circle the Hebrew words for **heaven** or **the heavens** in the three Hebrew lines from Isaiah above. How many words did you circle? _____

Underline the Hebrew words for **earth** or **the earth**. How many words did you circle? _____ *Hint:* Check out the photo caption on this page.

אֶרֶץ, שָׁמַיִם, וְצוֹפִים

Psst! The word הַצֹּפִים ("the scouts") appears in the Bible. Circle it below.

וַיִּרְאוּ הַצֹּפִים לְשָׁאוּל בְּגִבְעַת בִּנְיָמִן וְהִנֵּה הֶהָמוֹן נָמוֹג וַיֵּלֶךְ וַהֲלֹם.

(King) Saul's scouts in Gibeah of Benjamin saw masses of people scattering in all
directions. (1 Samuel 14:16)

Tic-Tac-Toe

Play Tic-Tac-Toe with a classmate. Take turns reading a word or phrase. If you are correct, lightly write an X or an O in pencil in that box.

אֱמֶת	וַאֲנַחְנוּ	גְּדֻלָּה	כּוֹרְעִים	לְפָנֶי	וְנֶאֱמַר
אֵין	בַּשָׁמַיִם	אֶחָד	הַכֹּל	שָׁם	לַאֲדוֹן
מֶלֶךְ מַלְכֵי הַמְּלָכִים	עֹז	אֲדָמָה	לְשַׁבֵּחַ	וּשְׁמוֹ	עָלֵינוּ

Clue to Cyberspace

Go down the steps of Masada by reading each line aloud and circling the words that do **not** appear in עָלֵינוּ.

1. עָלֵינוּ לְשַׁבֵּחַ לַאֲדוֹן יִשְׂרָאֵל הַכֹּל שֶׁלֹּא
2. עָשָׂנוּ כְּגוֹיֵי הָרַחֲמִים הָאֲרָצוֹת וַאֲנַחְנוּ כּוֹרְעִים
3. וּבָאָרֶץ וּמִשְׁתַּחֲוִים וּמוֹדִים לִפְנֵי מֶלֶךְ מַלְכֵי
4. הַמְּלָכִים וְנֶאֱמַר וְהָיָה דְּבָרִים בַּיּוֹם הַהוּא
5. יִהְיֶה הַגְּבוּרָה יְיָ אֶחָד וּשְׁמוֹ אֶחָד

On the lines below, write the first letter of each of the circled words to discover the Hebrew name of the desert in which Masada is located. Do not write any dots or vowels.

____ ____ ____ ____
‎ ָ ‎ ְ

Use this clue to score bonus points in the "Carnival Duck!" game in Level 5 on your computer.

Ben and Batya were visiting their cousins Oshrit and Gadi in Be'er Sheva. "Israel is a country full of hope—תִּקְוָה—just like it says in our national anthem," Oshrit explained. "Be'er Sheva is a great example. Lots of Jewish immigrants—עוֹלִים—settle here. Many come from Russia and Ethiopia, where they couldn't live freely as Jews. They made עֲלִיָּה in the hope that they could find work, raise families, and live proudly as Jews in Israel."

Who or what gives you courage and hope when you face a challenge, such as making a science project presentation or giving a speech? Why?

_____

_____

🛩 **Torah Travel** The Bible tells us that our patriarch Abraham's first purchase in the Land of Israel was a well—בְּאֵר—in the Negev Desert. He bought it from King Abimelech, with whom he swore an oath—שְׁבוּעָה.

...קָרָא לַמָּקוֹם הַהוּא בְּאֵר שָׁבַע כִּי שָׁם נִשְׁבְּעוּ שְׁנֵיהֶם.

"...called that place Be'er Sheva because the two of them swore an oath there."

(Genesis 21:31).

שְׁבוּעָה and שֶׁבַע are built on the same root—שבע. Locate and circle Be'er Sheva on the map on page 3.

Near the end of the service we say the קַדִּישׁ, a prayer we recite in memory of loved ones who have died. Surprisingly, the קַדִּישׁ doesn't mention death. Instead, it praises God and expresses our hope that God's laws of justice and loving-kindness will bring peace throughout the world.

Why, after a loved one dies, might it be comforting to say a prayer that says God is great and that we hope for a kinder, more peaceful world?

_____

Practice reading the קַדִּישׁ.

1. יִתְגַּדַּל וְיִתְקַדַּשׁ שְׁמֵהּ רַבָּא.

2. בְּעָלְמָא דִּי בְרָא כִרְעוּתֵהּ, וְיַמְלִיךְ מַלְכוּתֵהּ,

3. בְּחַיֵּיכוֹן וּבְיוֹמֵיכוֹן וּבְחַיֵּי דְכָל בֵּית יִשְׂרָאֵל,

4. בַּעֲגָלָא וּבִזְמַן קָרִיב. וְאִמְרוּ: אָמֵן.

5. יְהֵא שְׁמֵהּ רַבָּא מְבָרַךְ לְעָלַם וּלְעָלְמֵי עָלְמַיָּא.

1. May God's name be great and may it be made holy
2. in the world created according to God's will. May God rule
3. in our own lives and our own days, and in the life of all the house of Israel,
4. swiftly and soon. And say: Amen.
5. May God's great name be blessed forever and ever.

6. יִתְבָּרַךְ וְיִשְׁתַּבַּח, וְיִתְפָּאַר וְיִתְרוֹמַם וְיִתְנַשֵּׂא,

7. וְיִתְהַדָּר וְיִתְעַלֶּה וְיִתְהַלָּל שְׁמֵהּ דְּקֻדְשָׁא בְּרִיךְ הוּא,

8. לְעֵלָּא מִן כָּל בִּרְכָתָא וְשִׁירָתָא,

9. תֻּשְׁבְּחָתָא וְנֶחֱמָתָא, דַּאֲמִירָן בְּעָלְמָא. וְאִמְרוּ: אָמֵן.

6. Blessed, praised, glorified, exalted, extolled,
7. honored, magnified, and adored be the name of the blessed Holy One,
8. though God is beyond all the blessings, songs,
9. adorations, and consolations that are spoken in the world. And say: Amen.

10. יְהֵא שְׁלָמָא רַבָּא מִן שְׁמַיָּא,

11. וְחַיִּים עָלֵינוּ וְעַל כָּל יִשְׂרָאֵל. וְאִמְרוּ: אָמֵן.

12. עֹשֶׂה שָׁלוֹם בִּמְרוֹמָיו, הוּא יַעֲשֶׂה שָׁלוֹם עָלֵינוּ,

13. וְעַל כָּל יִשְׂרָאֵל. וְאִמְרוּ: אָמֵן.

10. *May there be great peace from heaven*
11. *and life for us and for all Israel. And say: Amen.*
12. *May God who makes peace in the heavens, make peace for us*
13. *and for all Israel. And say: Amen.*

The Hebrew-Aramaic Connection

Did you notice anything unusual about the language of the קַדִּישׁ? Most of the words are in Aramaic, a language that is similar to Hebrew. Aramaic was spoken by the Jews at the time of Ezra the prophet in the fifth century BCE and for about a thousand years after that.

The last two lines of the קַדִּישׁ are written in Hebrew. What is the name of another prayer in which those same two lines appear? *Hint:* Its English meaning is the

"Standing Prayer." _____

Many Aramaic words in the קַדִּישׁ are similar to Hebrew words that you already know. Be a world-class linguist and draw a line from each Hebrew word below to its related Aramaic word. *Hint:* Look for related roots.

ARAMAIC	HEBREW	
וְיַמְלִיךְ	שָׁלוֹם	1.
בְּרִיךְ	קָדוֹשׁ	2.
וְיִתְקַדַּשׁ	שָׁמַיִם	3.
שְׁלָמָא	יַמְלִיךְ	4.
בְּעָלְמָא	הַגָּדוֹל	5.
שְׁמַיָּא	בָּרוּךְ	6.
יִתְגַּדַּל	הָעוֹלָם	7.

Prayer Words

Practice reading these words from the קַדִּישׁ.

will be great	יִתְגַּדַּל
and will be holy	וְיִתְקַדַּשׁ
God's name	שְׁמֵהּ
in the world	בְּעָלְמָא
God's kingdom	מַלְכוּתֵהּ
the blessings	בִּרְכָתָא
peace	שְׁלָמָא

Getting to the Root of a Word

In the blank space next to each root below write a prayer word from above that is built on the same root.

1. בּרכ _____
2. מלכ _____
3. קדשׁ _____
4. שׁלמ _____

Bonus Points: Turn to the activity on page 62. Put a check next to each Hebrew and Aramaic word that is built on one of the roots below. *Hint:* ך is a final כ.

קדשׁ   בּרכ   שׁלמ   מלכ

Now, circle the root letters in each word that you checked.

 **Language Link**

The phrase בֵּית יִשְׂרָאֵל, in line 3 of the קַדִּיש, means **House of Israel.** בֵּית יִשְׂרָאֵל is not a place; it is the name of our people—the Jewish people. Many other Hebrew expressions that begin with the word בֵּית, meaning **house of**, *are* names of places. Here are just a few.

school (house of books)	בֵּית-סֵפֶר
cafe (house of coffee)	בֵּית-קָפֶה
hospital (house of the sick)	בֵּית-חוֹלִים
synagogue (house of assembly)	בֵּית-כְּנֶסֶת
court of law (house of law)	בֵּית-מִשְׁפָּט
factory (house of manufacturing)	בֵּית-חֲרֹשֶׁת

Hebrew Houses

Read the Hebrew phrases below then draw a line from each phrase to its illustration.

בֵּית-חֲרֹשֶׁת   בֵּית-כְּנֶסֶת   בֵּית-מִשְׁפָּט

בֵּית-חוֹלִים   בֵּית-קָפֶה   בֵּית-סֵפֶר

The Hebrew word meaning "house of" is _____.

More About the Kaddish

So far, you have learned about the Mourner's קַדִּישׁ. But there are other versions of the קַדִּישׁ. One is the חֲצִי קַדִּישׁ, which means "Half Kaddish," even though it is only slightly shorter than the Mourner's קַדִּישׁ. The קַדִּישׁ divides a prayer service just like a bell between classes divides a school day. It indicates the end of one section of the service and the start of the next.

In some congregations, only the mourners and those observing *yahrtzeit*—the anniversary of a loved one's death—stand as they recite the Mourner's קַדִּישׁ. In others, everyone stands.

We are not sure who wrote the קַדִּישׁ or when it was written. It probably evolved over several centuries. About eight hundred years ago the קַדִּישׁ became the prayer recited by mourners.

Traditionally we recite the קַדִּישׁ only in the presence of a מִנְיָן —a group of ten or more Jews who are at least of bar or bat mitzvah age. As the mourners chant the prayer, the congregation praises God, hoping their words of faith will comfort and strengthen the mourners.

What might be a good reason to recite the Mourner's קַדִּישׁ only in the presence of a מִנְיָן?

 **At the Root**

יִתְגַּדַּל means **May God's name be great**. The root of יִתְגַּדַּל is גדל.

The root גדל tells us that **great, big,** or **size** is part of a word's meaning.

Circle the root letters גדל in the words below.

גַּדֵּל   מִגְדָּל   גְּדוֹלָה   גָּדוֹל   גְּדוֹלוֹת   גַּדְלוּת   גַּדְלָנוּת

BIG or SMALL

If a building is BIG we say it is **גָדוֹל**, and if it is SMALL we call it **קָטָן**. Circle the building that matches the Hebrew phrase.

בֵּית-כְּנֶסֶת קָטָן

בֵּית-קָפֶּה גָדוֹל

בֵּית-סֵפֶר גָדוֹל

בֵּית-חוֹלִים קָטָן

What Do We Say?

On hearing that someone has died, it is a tradition for all people—mourners and non-mourners alike—to say:

בָּרוּךְ דַּיַן הָאֱמֶת.

Praised is the One True Judge.

Why do you think we say these words when we hear someone has died?

_____

_____

Taking Leave of Royalty

Practice reading the last two lines of the קַדִּישׁ.

1. עֹשֶׂה שָׁלוֹם בִּמְרוֹמָיו, הוּא יַעֲשֶׂה שָׁלוֹם

2. עָלֵינוּ, וְעַל כָּל יִשְׂרָאֵל. וְאִמְרוּ: אָמֵן.

1. May God who makes peace in the heavens, make peace

2. for us and for all Israel. And say, Amen.

עֹשֶׂה שָׁלוֹם is the same sentence that concludes the עֲמִידָה and appears near the end of בִּרְכַּת הַמָּזוֹן (Grace After Meals). When we say עֹשֶׂה שָׁלוֹם at the end of the קַדִּישׁ and the עֲמִידָה, it is a tradition to take three steps backward, then bow to the left, to the right, and to the front. It is as if we are leaving the presence of a great ruler.

Who is the ruler whose presence we are leaving? _____

If you could add another line about peace to עֹשֶׂה שָׁלוֹם, what would it be? Write it in English here:

_____

שָׁלוֹם

Putting It in ConTEXT

We pray for peace in every service. And we learn the value of peace and the importance of pursuing it. Here are three quotes from the Bible, the תָּנָ"ךְ—Torah, Prophets, and Writings—that speak of peace.

1. וְנָתַתִּי שָׁלוֹם בָּאָרֶץ וּשְׁכַבְתֶּם וְאֵין מַחֲרִיד... וְחֶרֶב לֹא־תַעֲבֹר בְּאַרְצְכֶם.

"I will grant peace throughout the land, so that you will lie down and not be troubled by anyone... No sword will cross through your land." (Leviticus 26:6)

2. ...וַאֲשַׁלֵּם נִחֻמִים לוֹ וְלַאֲבֵלָיו: בּוֹרֵא נוֹב [נִיב] שְׂפָתָיִם שָׁלוֹם שָׁלוֹם לָרָחוֹק וְלַקָּרוֹב אָמַר יְהוָֹה וּרְפָאתִיו.

"...and to the mourners among them I will give comfort. I who created speech [say] 'Peace, peace to the far and to the near,' says Adonai. And I will heal them." (Isaiah 57:18-19)

3. סוּר מֵרָע וַעֲשֵׂה־טוֹב בַּקֵּשׁ שָׁלוֹם וְרָדְפֵהוּ.

"Steer clear of evil and do good; seek peace and pursue it." (Psalms 34:15)

Write שָׁלוֹם below the symbols for peace. Then create your own peace symbol.

_____

_____

P R A Y E R   P U Z Z L E

Complete the puzzle by writing the Hebrew word from the word bank in the box below that is related to the word from the קַדִּישׁ. Do not include the vowels or any other marks that look like dots.

Across

1. בְּעָלְמָא

3. דַּאֲמִירָן

5. וְיִתְקַדַּשׁ

Down

1. יִתְגַּדַּל

2. שְׁמַיָּא

4. מַלְכוּתֵהּ

Word bank

מַלְכוּתְךָ

הַגְדָּלָה

הָעוֹלָם

בִּקְדֻשָּׁתוֹ

בַּשָּׁמַיִם

הַנֶּאֱמָרִים

Clue to Cyberspace

Sharpen your Hebrew. Read the following Hebrew and Aramaic words from the קַדִּישׁ. Circle only the Hebrew words. How many words did you circle?_____

Then draw a line to connect each of the *Hebrew* words to אֶרֶץ יִשְׂרָאֵל. *Hint:* Aramaic words often end with א.

בְּעָלְמָא	עָלֵינוּ	הוּא	רַבָּא
וְאִמְרוּ	תֻּשְׁבְּחָתָא	וְשִׁירָתָא	בִּרְכָתָא
עֹשֶׂה	שְׁלָמָא	וְנֶחֱמָתָא	יַעֲשֶׂה
שָׁלוֹם	וְחַיִּים	וְעַל	שְׁמַיָּא

Now find and copy the Hebrew word that is also the name of a prayer. _____

Place this clue in its correct spot in the "Stampede" game in Level 6 on your computer.

It was like no other school day. Ben and Batya were on a class trip to Tiberias, a city on the western shore of Lake Kinneret—יַם כִּנֶּרֶת. "Tiberias—טְבֶרְיָה—was built about 2,000 years ago," their teacher Eli explained. (Yes, Israeli students call teachers by their first names!) "After the Temple was destroyed, טְבֶרְיָה became a center of Jewish learning and culture. It's where our sages developed the collection of Jewish laws called the Palestinian Talmud." ▬▬

"I learned that Tiberias was also the home of the ancient high court—the Sanhedrin," Batya said to Ben. "It's one of Judaism's holiest cities. Just thinking about its history, not to mention today's swim party at יַם כִּנֶּרֶת, feels awesome times ten."

✈ **Torah Travel** Tradition teaches that טְבֶרְיָה was built on the remains of the city of Rakkat, which is mentioned in the Bible:

וְעָרֵי מִבְצָר הַצִּדִּים צֵר וְחַמַּת רַקַּת וְכִנָּרֶת.

"And the fortified cities were Ziddim, Zeir, and Ḥammat, Rakkat, and Kinneret."
(Joshua 19:35)

Locate and circle טְבֶרְיָה and יַם כִּנֶּרֶת on the map on page 3.

Describe a time or place that fills you with awe and wonder.

_____

_____

On Shabbat morning, many congregations sing אֲדוֹן עוֹלָם or אֵין כֵּאלֹהֵינוּ (or both!) as part of the prayer service's conclusion. Both hymns describe God as our Sovereign and Ruler, an awesome power beyond compare. We sing both with spirit and joy. You will learn both of these hymns in this chapter.

God is not the leader of a country or even human. So what do we mean when we say that God is our Sovereign and Ruler?

You're the Greatest

אֵין כֵּאלֹהֵינוּ praises God as having no equal.

Practice reading אֵין כֵּאלֹהֵינוּ.

אֵין כַּאדוֹנֵינוּ,	1. אֵין כֵּאלֹהֵינוּ,
אֵין כְּמוֹשִׁיעֵנוּ.	2. אֵין כְּמַלְכֵּנוּ,
מִי כַאדוֹנֵינוּ,	3. מִי כֵאלֹהֵינוּ,
מִי כְמוֹשִׁיעֵנוּ.	4. מִי כְמַלְכֵּנוּ,
נוֹדֶה לַאדוֹנֵינוּ,	5. נוֹדֶה לֵאלֹהֵינוּ,
נוֹדֶה לְמוֹשִׁיעֵנוּ.	6. נוֹדֶה לְמַלְכֵּנוּ,
בָּרוּךְ אֲדוֹנֵינוּ,	7. בָּרוּךְ אֱלֹהֵינוּ,
בָּרוּךְ מוֹשִׁיעֵנוּ.	8. בָּרוּךְ מַלְכֵּנוּ,
אַתָּה הוּא אֲדוֹנֵינוּ,	9. אַתָּה הוּא אֱלֹהֵינוּ,
אַתָּה הוּא מוֹשִׁיעֵנוּ.	10. אַתָּה הוּא מַלְכֵּנוּ,

1. There is none like our God,   There is none like our Sovereign,
2. There is none like our Ruler,   There is none like our Savior.
3. Who is like our God?   Who is like our Sovereign?
4. Who is like our Ruler?   Who is like our Savior?
5. We will give thanks to our God,   We will give thanks to our Sovereign,
6. We will give thanks to our Ruler, We will give thanks to our Savior.
7. Blessed is our God,   Blessed is our Sovereign,
8. Blessed is our Ruler,   Blessed is our Savior.
9. You are our God,   You are our Sovereign,
10. You are our Ruler,   You are our Savior.

Prayer Words

Practice reading these words from אֵין כֵּאלֹהֵינוּ.

English	Hebrew
there is none like	אֵין כְּ–
who is like	מִי כְ–
we will give thanks to	נוֹדֶה לְ–
You (God) are	אַתָּה הוּא
our God	אֱלֹהֵינוּ
our Sovereign	אֲדוֹנֵינוּ
our Ruler	מַלְכֵּנוּ
our Savior	מוֹשִׁיעֵנוּ

God's Majesty

Under each crown, write the English meaning of the word in the crown.

_____ _____ _____ _____

Bonus points: In each of the four Hebrew words, circle the word ending that means **our**.

With a partner, find and underline the Hebrew word below that is related to נוֹדֶה לְ-.

שָׁלוֹם   תּוֹדָה   יִשְׂרָאֵל   תּוֹרָה

Now, use this word to thank your partner for working with you.

At the Heart of It All

When we sing אֵין כֵּאלֹהֵינוּ, we describe God in four ways—אֱלֹהֵינוּ (our God), אֲדוֹנֵינוּ (our Sovereign), מַלְכֵּנוּ (our Ruler), and מוֹשִׁיעֵנוּ (our Savior). Each is built on a name of God. At first, you may not recognize God's name because when a word has a prefix or suffix added, it can change the word's vowels or cause it to lose a final letter.

Connect each name of God in column 1 to its related word from אֵין כֵּאלֹהֵינוּ in column 2.

Then write the English meaning for the words in column 1 in the blank spaces.

2		1
אֱלֹהֵינוּ	_____	מֶלֶךְ
אֲדוֹנֵינוּ	_____	מוֹשִׁיעַ
מוֹשִׁיעֵנוּ	_____	אֱלֹהִים
מַלְכֵּנוּ	_____	אָדוֹן

There are many other ways to describe God. For example, other prayers call God יוֹצְרֵנוּ (our Creator), אָבִינוּ (our Parent; literally, our Father), and רוֹעֵנוּ (our Shepherd).

Why do you think we describe God in different ways? _____

_____

How would *you* describe God? God is our/my _____

Which did you choose, "our" or "my"? Why? _____

_____

Prefix Please

There Is None Like אֵין כּ–

אֵין means **there is none**.

כּ– is a prefix that means **like**.

אֵין כּ– means _____ .

Circle the word and prefix that mean **there is none like** in the lines below.

אֵין כֵּאלֹהֵינוּ   אֵין כַּאדוֹנֵינוּ

אֵין כְּמַלְכֵּנוּ   אֵין כְּמוֹשִׁיעֵנוּ

Who Is Like מִי כ–

מִי means **who is**.

כ– is a prefix that means **like**.

Circle the word and prefix that mean **who is like** in the lines below.

מִי כֵאלֹהֵינוּ   מִי כַאדוֹנֵינוּ

מִי כְמַלְכֵּנוּ   מִי כְמוֹשִׁיעֵנוּ

We Will Give Thanks to נוֹדֶה ל–

נוֹדֶה means **we will give thanks**.

ל– is a prefix that means _____ .

Circle the word and prefix that mean **we will give thanks to** in the lines below.

נוֹדֶה לֵאלֹהֵינוּ   נוֹדֶה לַאדוֹנֵינוּ

נוֹדֶה לְמַלְכֵּנוּ   נוֹדֶה לְמוֹשִׁיעֵנוּ

Crack the Code

אֵין כֵּאלֹהֵינוּ is an acrostic—a poem in which a hidden message is spelled out by stringing together the first letter of each verse or, in this case, every other line.

Turn to page 74 and follow these directions to crack the code of the אֵין כֵּאלֹהֵינוּ acrostic.

1. Circle אֵין each time it appears.
2. Underline מִי each time it appears.
3. Put a box around נוֹדֶה each time it appears.
4. To spell out a new secret word, in the space below write the first letter of each of the following words from אֵין כֵּאלֹהֵינוּ:

נוֹדֶה   מִי   אֵין

(Remember: נ at the end of a word is written ן.)

_____   _____   _____
           ..   ָ

When do we say this word?

_____

The first word in each of the last two verses of אֵין כֵּאלֹהֵינוּ are בָּרוּךְ and אַתָּה. Jewish tradition tells us that by saying a blessing's ending (אָמֵן) followed by a blessing's beginning (בָּרוּךְ אַתָּה) we are reminded that our praise of God should go on forever.

אָמֵן!

And Now, a Word about Israel

Some synagogues recite an additional verse at the end of אֵין כֵּאלֹהֵינוּ. It is a reminder of the days when our people made sacrifices and burned incense in Jerusalem's Temple.

אַתָּה הוּא שֶׁהִקְטִירוּ אֲבוֹתֵינוּ לְפָנֶיךָ אֵת קְטֹרֶת הַסַּמִּים.

It was in front of You that our ancestors burned the incense.

Circle the Hebrew word above that ends in the suffix meaning **our**.

Bonus Points: What does the word you circled mean? _____

Can you name two of אֲבוֹתֵינוּ? Write their names in Hebrew or English.

_____   _____

Underline the Hebrew word above that means **You**.

Crazy Bonus Points: Draw a squiggly line under the two Hebrew words above that share the same root.

Off the Charts Bonus Points: What are the root letters in the two words?

_____ _____ _____

יְרוּשָׁלַיִם

 **Language Link**

The last verse of אֵין כֵּאלֹהֵינוּ begins with the phrase אַתָּה הוּא, which means **You (God) are**. When the words are used individually, they are two separate pronouns meaning **you** and **he**. Below are the masculine and feminine forms of Hebrew singular pronouns.

F	M
אֲנִי	אֲנִי
אַתְּ	אַתָּה
הִיא	הוּא

Join Ben and Batya at יַם כִּנֶּרֶת. They and their classmates want to introduce themselves to you.

Now let's see who you remember. Fill in the blanks with הִיא, הוּא, אֲנִי, or the right name.

בָּתְיָה _____   _____ הוּא   בֵּן_____   _____ הִיא דָּוִד_____   שָׂרָה _____

Can you answer this question in Hebrew?

אֲנִי מִי אַתָּה/אַתְּ? _____

77

God of Eternity

אַדוֹן עוֹלָם praises God as having no equal, just as אֵין כֵּאלֹהֵינוּ does. In addition, it says that the God of the whole universe is also my personal God, who cares about me.

Practice reading אֲדוֹן עוֹלָם.

1. אֲדוֹן עוֹלָם אֲשֶׁר מָלַךְ, בְּטֶרֶם כָּל יְצִיר נִבְרָא.

2. לְעֵת נַעֲשָׂה בְחֶפְצוֹ כֹּל, אֲזַי מֶלֶךְ שְׁמוֹ נִקְרָא.

3. וְאַחֲרֵי כִּכְלוֹת הַכֹּל, לְבַדּוֹ יִמְלוֹךְ נוֹרָא.

4. וְהוּא הָיָה, וְהוּא הוֶה, וְהוּא יִהְיֶה, בְּתִפְאָרָה.

5. וְהוּא אֶחָד וְאֵין שֵׁנִי, לְהַמְשִׁיל לוֹ לְהַחְבִּירָה.

6. בְּלִי רֵאשִׁית בְּלִי תַכְלִית, וְלוֹ הָעֹז וְהַמִּשְׂרָה.

7. וְהוּא אֵלִי וְחַי גֹּאֲלִי, וְצוּר חֶבְלִי בְּעֵת צָרָה.

8. וְהוּא נִסִּי וּמָנוֹס לִי, מְנָת כּוֹסִי בְּיוֹם אֶקְרָא.

9. בְּיָדוֹ אַפְקִיד רוּחִי, בְּעֵת אִישַׁן וְאָעִירָה.

10. וְעִם רוּחִי גְוִיָּתִי, יְיָ לִי וְלֹא אִירָא.

1. *Sovereign of the universe who ruled before any being was created,*
2. *at the time when everything was created according to God's will, then God was called Ruler.*
3. *After all else ends, God alone will rule in majesty.*
4. *God was, God is, and God will be in glory.*
5. *God is One and there is no one who is God's peer or who can join with God.*
6. *Without a beginning, without an end, power and dominion are God's.*
7. *God is my God and my living Redeemer, and my Rock in times of trouble and distress.*
8. *God is my banner and my refuge, the portion of my cup on the day I call.*
9. *I entrust my spirit into God's hand, when I sleep and when I wake.*
10. *And with my spirit and my body, Adonai is with me and I shall not be afraid.*

Prayer Words

Practice reading these words from אֲדוֹן עוֹלָם.

Sovereign	אֲדוֹן
(God) was	הָיָה
(God) is	הוֶֹה
(God) will be	יִהְיֶה
without a beginning	בְּלִי רֵאשִׁית
without an end	בְּלִי תַכְלִית
my Redeemer	גּאֲֹלִי

Wish for the World

Write the Hebrew word for each English meaning.

without a beginning   ___ ___ ◯ ___ ___   ___ ___ ___ .1

without an end   ___ ___ ◯ ___ ___   ___ ___ ___ .2

Sovereign   ___ ◯ ___ ___ .3

Now copy the circled letters to reveal our greatest wish for the world.

ם ___   ___ ___   ___ ___
         ָ

Was, Is, Will Be!

Why do you think אֲדוֹן עוֹלָם says of God: הָיָה, הוֶֹה, יִהְיֶה (was, is, and will be)?

_____

Putting It in ConTEXT

In אֲדוֹן עוֹלָם אֵין כֵּאלֹהֵינוּ we speak as a community, so we say "our God." But in
we speak as individuals, so we say "my God." In fact, the last four lines of אֲדוֹן עוֹלָם
say "my" nine times, "I" four times, and "me" once.

Why do you think that in some prayers we speak as a community and in others we
speak as individuals? _____

_____

The last four lines of אֲדוֹן עוֹלָם express similar thoughts to Psalms 23:1–4.

1. יְהוָֹה רֹעִי

2. נַפְשִׁי יְשׁוֹבֵב יַנְחֵנִי בְמַעְגְּלֵי־צֶדֶק

3. גַּם כִּי־אֵלֵךְ בְּגֵיא צַלְמָוֶת לֹא־אִירָא רָע כִּי־אַתָּה עִמָּדִי

4. שִׁבְטְךָ וּמִשְׁעַנְתֶּךָ הֵמָּה יְנַחֲמֻנִי.

1. Adonai is my Shepherd

2. (God) restores my spirit, (God) guides me in righteous paths

3. Though I walk through the valley of the shadow of death, I fear no evil, for
   You are with me

4. Your rod and Your staff, they comfort me.

If God is not a person, how can God protect and comfort us? _____

_____

Write a poem, blessing, or statement describing what guides and comforts you at
difficult moments. _____

_____

_____

_____

Name that Tune

We conclude the Shabbat prayer service with a lively hymn, often singing
אֲדוֹן עוֹלָם to the tune of a fun song such as "Deep in the Heart of Texas" or
"Yankee Doodle." When a holiday falls on Shabbat, we might sing אֲדוֹן עוֹלָם to
the melody of a song for that holiday.

Match each holiday below with the tune we might use for אֲדוֹן עוֹלָם when the
holiday falls on Shabbat.

TUNE		**HOLIDAY**
מָעוֹז צוּר		פֶּסַח
דַּיֵּנוּ		4 בְּיוּלִי
"גַּד בְּלֶס אֲמֶרִיקָה"		חֲנֻכָּה

Clue to Cyberspace

Meet Ben and Batya in טְבֶרְיָה. Then jog around יַם כִּנֶּרֶת as you read each Hebrew word.

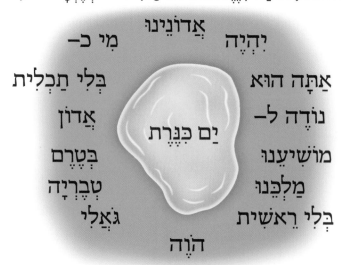

אֲדוֹנֵינוּ
מִי כְ–   יִהְיֶה
בְּלִי תַכְלִית   אַתָּה הוּא
אָדוֹן   נוֹדֶה ל–
יַם כִּנֶּרֶת
בְּטֶרֶם   מוֹשִׁיעֵנוּ
טְבֶרְיָה   מַלְכֵּנוּ
גֹּאֲלִי   בְּלִי רֵאשִׁית
הֹוֶה

Circle the word that is part of the name of the prayer we are learning. Place this
clue in its correct space in the "Stampede" game in Level 7 on your computer.

Batya and Ben's Big Day!

"The best," Batya gasped as she and Ben completed the final rehearsal of their haftarah. They had chanted the הַפְטָרָה and בִּרְכוֹת perfectly! "Well, tomorrow is the big day, our bat and bar mitzvah, and we are ready for it," said Ben. "I'm glad we are having the prayer service and party in _____.

(name a city in Israel)

It's my favorite city in Israel because

_____

_____"

"Yup. It's the perfect place," Batya agreed. "I've had such a great time studying and traveling in Israel this year. It's hard to believe that in just two weeks we'll be back home. Wait 'til I tell our friends about the time we

_____

_____."

(describe a fun thing to do in Israel, like a swim party at the Kinneret)

"Don't worry. This is just one of many trips we'll take to Israel. Our synagogue and youth group have teen summer programs in Israel. If we start lobbying mom and dad now, there's a good chance we can come back in a few years," Ben said.

"Sounds like a plan," agreed Batya. "But now, we need to focus on our big day tomorrow. So let's practice the Sheheḥeyanu blessing."

Please join Ben and Batya in practicing the שֶׁהֶחֱיָנוּ.

בָּרוּךְ אַתָּה, יְיָ אֱלֹהֵינוּ, מֶלֶךְ הָעוֹלָם, שֶׁהֶחֱיָנוּ וְקִיְּמָנוּ וְהִגִּיעָנוּ לַזְּמַן הַזֶּה.

Praised are you, Adonai our God, Ruler of the world, who has given us life, sustained us, and enabled us to reach this time.

My **Big Day**

I am a student at _____.
(name of religious school)

I will celebrate becoming a _____ mitzvah on _____, _____.
(bar/bat)   (day of the week)   (date)

My פָּרָשָׁה is about _____.

My הַפְטָרָה is about _____.

My מִצְוָה project may be about _____.

My prayer service will be held at _____.

What I most look forward to about becoming a bar/bat mitzvah is _____

_____ because _____

_____.

There is much I have learned about Judaism and more that I will continue to learn, and so I offer this blessing of gratitude.

אַתָּה חוֹנֵן לְאָדָם דַּעַת, וּמְלַמֵּד לֶאֱנוֹשׁ בִּינָה. חָנֵּנוּ מֵאִתְּךָ
דֵּעָה, בִּינָה וְהַשְׂכֵּל. בָּרוּךְ אַתָּה, יְיָ, חוֹנֵן הַדָּעַת.

You graciously gave humans the ability to learn, teaching us wisdom. Grant us intelligence, wisdom, and understanding. Praised are You, Adonai, who graciously grants us the power to learn. (from the Amidah)

Kol Yisrael Wrap-Up

Know Your Roots

Be a super sleuth and uncover the roots of the Hebrew words. Write each root at the base of the tree. Look in the grass to find the English meaning related to this root. Copy the English word below the Hebrew root.

מַלְכוּתוֹ
מֶלֶךְ
מַלְכֵּנוּ

נְקַדֵּשׁ
קִדְּשָׁנוּ
וְיִתְקַדַּשׁ

חַיִּים
חַי
מְחַיֶּה

בָּרוּךְ
בְּרָכָה
בִּרְכָתָא

וְאָהַבְתָּ
אַהֲבָה
אַהֲבַת

love   bless, praise   holiness   life   rule

84

שָׁלוֹם
בִּשְׁלוֹמֶךְ
שְׁלָמָא

הָרַחֲמִים
בְּרַחֲמִים
רַחֵם

וְהַגְּבוּרָה
הַגִּבּוֹר
גְּבוּרוֹת

יִתְגַּדַּל
הַגְּדֻלָה
הַגָּדוֹל

הַנֶּאֱמָרִים
הָאוֹמֵר
וְאִמְרוּ

wholeness   compassion, mercy   say   power, might   great, big

How does knowing these key roots help you to understand prayers?

_____

_____

Following Orders

Batya and Ben are working on their computer to plan a Shabbat retreat. Each prayer is on a separate document. Help them plan services for the retreat by numbering the prayers, beginning with Shabbat morning, according to the order in which they are recited.

Challenge: Name two additional prayers that Ben and Batya could add to their list.

_____   _____

3-2-1 Action!

Ben and Batya are making a film about leading Shabbat services. They filmed a silent video and then made recordings of prayers being chanted. Write the number of each prayer next to its matching action to help Ben and Batya sync the chanting of the prayers with the video.

_____ close eyes or cover eyes with hand	1.	אָבוֹת וְאִמָּהוֹת
_____ take three steps backward then forward	2.	קְדוּשָׁה
_____ come up to the bimah for an aliyah	3.	וְזֹאת הַתּוֹרָה
_____ raise the Torah for everyone to see	4.	בִּרְכוֹת הַתּוֹרָה
_____ rise up on toes three times	5.	עָלֵינוּ
_____ bend knees and bow during the prayer	6.	שְׁמַע

Describe one way that these actions can make prayer more meaningful.

_____

_____

סִדוּר

Abundant Blessings

With a partner take turns reading the blessings below. Write the number of each illustration next to its matching blessing. Then answer the questions on page 89.

—— בָּרוּךְ אַתָּה, יְיָ אֱלֹהֵינוּ, מֶלֶךְ הָעוֹלָם, אֲשֶׁר קִדְּשָׁנוּ בְּמִצְוֹתָיו וְצִוָּנוּ לִקְבֹּעַ מְזוּזָה.

—— בָּרוּךְ אַתָּה, יְיָ אֱלֹהֵינוּ, מֶלֶךְ הָעוֹלָם, בּוֹרֵא פְּרִי הָאֲדָמָה.

—— בָּרוּךְ אַתָּה, יְיָ אֱלֹהֵינוּ, מֶלֶךְ הָעוֹלָם, בּוֹרֵא מִינֵי בְשָׂמִים.

—— בָּרוּךְ אַתָּה, יְיָ אֱלֹהֵינוּ, מֶלֶךְ הָעוֹלָם, בּוֹרֵא מִינֵי מְזוֹנוֹת.

—— בָּרוּךְ אַתָּה, יְיָ אֱלֹהֵינוּ, מֶלֶךְ הָעוֹלָם, אֲשֶׁר קִדְּשָׁנוּ בְּמִצְוֹתָיו, וְצִוָּנוּ לְהַדְלִיק נֵר שֶׁל שַׁבָּת.

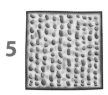

—— בָּרוּךְ אַתָּה, יְיָ אֱלֹהֵינוּ, מֶלֶךְ הָעוֹלָם, אֲשֶׁר קִדְּשָׁנוּ בְּמִצְוֹתָיו וְצִוָּנוּ עַל אֲכִילַת מַצָּה.

בָּרוּךְ אַתָּה, יְיָ אֱלֹהֵינוּ, מֶלֶךְ הָעוֹלָם, הַמּוֹצִיא לֶחֶם מִן הָאָרֶץ. _____ **7**

בָּרוּךְ אַתָּה, יְיָ אֱלֹהֵינוּ, מֶלֶךְ הָעוֹלָם, בּוֹרֵא פְּרִי הַגָּפֶן. _____ **8**

בָּרוּךְ אַתָּה, יְיָ אֱלֹהֵינוּ, מֶלֶךְ הָעוֹלָם, אֲשֶׁר קִדְּשָׁנוּ בְּמִצְוֹתָיו וְצִוָּנוּ לֵישֵׁב בַּסֻּכָּה. _____ **9**

בָּרוּךְ אַתָּה, יְיָ אֱלֹהֵינוּ, מֶלֶךְ הָעוֹלָם, אֲשֶׁר קִדְּשָׁנוּ בְּמִצְוֹתָיו וְצִוָּנוּ לְהַדְלִיק נֵר שֶׁל חֲנֻכָּה. _____ **10**

בָּרוּךְ אַתָּה, יְיָ אֱלֹהֵינוּ, מֶלֶךְ הָעוֹלָם, בּוֹרֵא פְּרִי הָעֵץ. _____ **11**

בָּרוּךְ אַתָּה, יְיָ אֱלֹהֵינוּ, מֶלֶךְ הָעוֹלָם, אֲשֶׁר קִדְּשָׁנוּ בְּמִצְוֹתָיו וְצִוָּנוּ לִשְׁמֹעַ קוֹל שׁוֹפָר. _____ **12**

Write the four Hebrew words that identify a blessing we say when performing a mitzvah.

_____

How many blessings of mitzvah did you find? _____

What's the Big Idea?

Read the list of prayers below. Then complete the activities that follow.

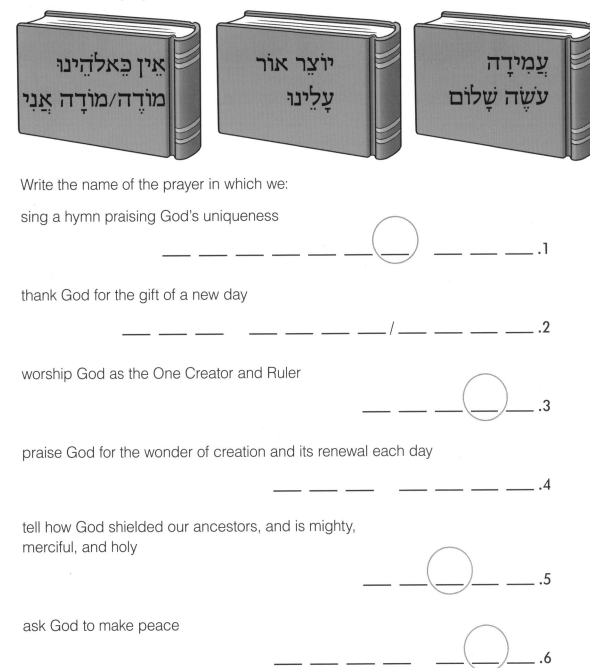

אֵין כֵּאלֹהֵינוּ
מוֹדֶה/מוֹדָה אֲנִי

יוֹצֵר אוֹר
עָלֵינוּ

עֲמִידָה
עֹשֶׂה שָׁלוֹם

Write the name of the prayer in which we:

sing a hymn praising God's uniqueness

— — — — — —◯— — — — .1

thank God for the gift of a new day

— — — — — — —/— — — — .2

worship God as the One Creator and Ruler

— — —◯— .3

praise God for the wonder of creation and its renewal each day

— — — — — — — .4

tell how God shielded our ancestors, and is mighty, merciful, and holy

— —◯— — .5

ask God to make peace

— — — — —◯— .6

Continue with the next list of prayers.

הַבְדָלָה
בִּרְכוֹת הַתּוֹרָה

בָּרְכוּ
בִּרְכַּת הַמָּזוֹן

מִי כָמֹכָה
וְאָהַבְתָּ

Write the name of the prayer in which we:

express gratitude for our freedom

— — — — — — — .7

praise God for giving us
the Torah

— ◯ — — — — — — — — — .8

are taught to show our love for God by following God's mitzvot

— — — ◯— — .9

thank God for a meal we have eaten

— — — — — — — — — .10

praise God for separating Shabbat from the rest
of the week

— ◯ — — — .11

announce that the prayer service is beginning

— — — — .12

Now copy the letters from the circles to the lines below to write a name for the Jewish people. *Hint:* It's also the name of this book!

— — — — — — —
  ◌ֵ   ◌ָ   ◌ְ   ◌ִ   ◌ָ

Speak Up

Read the Hebrew words and phrases aloud. Then circle the word or phrase that we say on each of the following occasions:

1. after hearing a blessing	אָמֵן	יְיַשֵׁר כֹּחַ
2. on Shabbat	לְשָׁנָה הַבָּאָה בִּירוּשָׁלַיִם	שַׁבָּת שָׁלוֹם
3. in the morning	בְּבַקָשָׁה	בֹּקֶר טוֹב
4. during Sukkot	שָׁנָה טוֹבָה וּמְתוּקָה	חַג שָׂמֵחַ
5. to welcome guests	בְּרוּכִים הַבָּאִים	עֶרֶב טוֹב
6. before going to sleep	לַיְלָה טוֹב	שָׁבוּעַ טוֹב
7. on receiving a gift	לְחַיִּים	תּוֹדָה
8. when meeting a stranger	מַה שְׁמֵךְ?	רְפוּאָה שְׁלֵמָה

Copy two phrases or words you have *not* circled and describe an occasion when you might say or hear these words.

1. _____

2. _____

Family Facts

Circle the name of the husband, wife, or wives of the ancestor in **bold** on each line below.

יִצְחָק	אַבְרָהָם	אַהֲרֹון	מֹשֶׁה	**שָׂרָה** .1
בַּת־שֶׁבַע	לֵאָה	רִבְקָה	מִרְיָם	**יִצְחָק** .2
דְּבוֹרָה	לֵאָה	שָׂרָה	רָחֵל	**יַעֲקֹב** .3

Underline the Hebrew name of Abraham and Sarah's son. Put a rectangle around the name of their grandson.

Why do you think the names of the אָבוֹת and אִמָּהוֹת are still popular for babies born nowadays?

_____

Best Wishes

Read each prayer phrase aloud with a partner.

1. עֹשֶׂה שָׁלוֹם בִּמְרוֹמָיו

2. עֹשֶׂה שָׁלוֹם וּבוֹרֵא אֶת הַכֹּל

3. הוּא יַעֲשֶׂה שָׁלוֹם עָלֵינוּ וְעַל כָּל יִשְׂרָאֵל

4. הַמְבָרֵךְ אֶת עַמּוֹ יִשְׂרָאֵל בַּשָׁלוֹם

5. שָׁלוֹם רָב עַל יִשְׂרָאֵל עַמְּךָ

Circle the word that appears most frequently in these lines. What does it mean?

How many times did you circle this word? _____

Why do you think this word appears so frequently in our prayers?

_____

_____

Mitzvot in Action

Prayers can remind us to perform מִצְוֹת and try to make the world a better place. Draw a line to connect the Hebrew for each מִצְוָה to its English meaning.

acts of loving-kindness   צְדָקָה

Jewish learning   שְׁלוֹם בַּיִת

peace in the home   חֲסָדִים טוֹבִים

tzedakah, justice, righteousnes   תַּלְמוּד תּוֹרָה

Choose a מִצְוָה from the list above. Write it here. _____

Now draw a picture to illustrate this מִצְוָה.

מִלּוֹן

א

אַב, אָב	parent, father
אָבוֹת	fathers (patriarchs, ancestors)
אֲבוֹתֵינוּ	our fathers
אַבְרָהָם	Abraham
אֲדוֹן	Sovereign
אֲדוֹנֵינוּ	our Sovereign
אֲדָמָה	earth
אוֹר	light
אֶחָד	one
אֵין	(there is) none
אֵין כְּ–	there is none like
אֲכִילַת	eating (of)
אֵל	God
אֱלֹהֵי	God of
אֱלֹהֵינוּ	our God
אִמָּהוֹת	mothers (matriarchs, ancestors)
אִמּוֹתֵינוּ	our mothers
אָמֵן	Amen
אֱמֶת	truth
אֲנִי	I
אֵשׁ	fire
אֲשֶׁר	that, which
אַתָּה	you (for a boy or man)
אַתָּה הוּא	You (God) are
אֶתְרוֹג	etrog

ב

(בְּ)אַהֲבָה	(in/with) love
בָּאֵלִם	among the gods (that other nations worship)
בֶּאֱמֶת	in truth
בְּדִבְרֵי	in the words of
בְּדִבְרֵיהֶם	with their words
בּוֹרֵא	who creates
בַּזְּמַן הַזֶּה	at this time
בְּחֶסֶד	with kindness
בָּחַר	chose (choosing)
בְּיַד	by the hand of
בֵּיתֶךָ	your house
בְּכָל־דּוֹר וָדוֹר	from generation to generation
בְּלִי רֵאשִׁית	without a beginning
בְּלִי תַכְלִית	without an end
בְּמִצְוֹתָיו	with God's commandments
בָּנוּ	us
בְּנֵי יִשְׂרָאֵל	Children of Israel
בַּסֻּכָּה	in the sukkah
בְּעֵינֶיךָ	in Your eyes
בַּעַל גְּבוּרוֹת	Powerful One
בְּעָלְמָא	in the world
בַּקֹּדֶשׁ	in holiness
בִּקְדֻשָּׁתוֹ	in (God's) holiness
בָּרוּךְ	blessed, praised
בְּרַחֲמִים	with compassion, mercy
בְּרָכָה, בְּרָכוֹת	blessing(s)
בְּרָכָה, בְּרָכוֹת	blessing(s)
שֶׁל מִצְוָה	when we do a mitzvah
בָּרְכוּ	bless! praise!
בִּרְכָתָא	the blessings
בִּרְכַּת הַמָּזוֹן	the blessing after a meal, Grace after Meals
בִּשְׁלוֹמֶךָ	with Your peace
בַּשָּׁמַיִם	in heaven
בְּשָׂמִים	spices

ג

גֹּאֲלִי	my Redeemer
גִּבּוֹר	mighty, powerful
גְּבוּרוֹת	powers
גַּדְּלוּ	glorify
גָּדְלְךָ	Your greatness

ד

דְּרָכֶיהָ	its ways, its paths

ה

הָאֲדָמָה	the earth
הָאוֹמֵר	the One who says
הַבְדָּלָה	separation
הַגִּבּוֹר	the mighty
הַגָּדוֹל	the great
הַגְּדֻלָּה	the greatness
הַגָּפֶן	the vine
הֹוֶה	(God) is
הַזֶּה	this
הַזָּן	who feeds
הָיָה	(God) was
הַכּוֹכָבִים	the stars
הַכֹּל	of all
הַלַּיְלָה	the night
הַמְּאוֹרוֹת	the heavenly lights
הַמַּבְדִּיל	who separates
הַמְבָרֵךְ	who blesses
הַמְבֹרָךְ	who is to be blessed, praised
הַמּוֹצִיא	who brings forth
הַנֶּאֱמָן	the One who is faithful
הַנֶּאֱמָרִים	spoken
הָעוֹלָם	the world
הָעַמִּים	the nations
הָרַחֲמִים	merciful, the mercy

ו

וְאָהַבְתָּ	you shall love
וְאַהֲבַת חֶסֶד	and a love of kindness
וְאִמְרוּ	and say
וַאֲנַחְנוּ	and we
וּבָאָרֶץ	and on earth
וּבוֹרֵא	and creates
(וּבְ)רָצוֹן	(and in/with) favor
וְהַגְּבוּרָה	and the power
וְהַנּוֹרָא	and the awesome
וְזֹאת	and this is
וְחַיֵּי	and life (of)

food	מָזוֹן
mezuzot	מְזוּזוֹת
gives life	מְחַיֶּה
who is like	מִי כְ–
who is like You	מִי כָמְכָה
from Jerusalem	מִירוּשָׁלַיִם
from all	מִכָּל
ruler, king	מֶלֶךְ
God's kingdom	מַלְכוּתֵהּ
Your sovereignty	מַלְכוּתְךָ
Ruler of the rulers of rulers	מֶלֶךְ מַלְכֵי הַמְּלָכִים
our Ruler	מַלְכֵּנוּ
brings on the evening	מַעֲרִיב עֲרָבִים
matzah	מַצָּה
commandment(s)	מִצְוָה, מִצְוֹת
out of Zion, from Zion	מִצִּיּוֹן
maror/bitter herbs	מָרוֹר
Moses	מֹשֶׁה

נ
English	Hebrew
prophets	נְבִיאִים
Your prophet	נְבִיאֶךָ
we will give thanks to	נוֹדֶה לְ–
gives	נוֹתֵן
miracles	נִסִּים
pleasantness	נֹעַם
your soul	נַפְשְׁךָ
let us sanctify, make holy	נְקַדֵּשׁ
candle, light	נֵר

ע
English	Hebrew
his (God's) servant	עַבְדוֹ
helper	עוֹזֵר
eternal, world	עוֹלָם
eternal	עוֹלָמִים
strength	עֹז
supreme	עֶלְיוֹן
for us, on us, it is upon us (our duty)	עָלֵינוּ

English	Hebrew
Israel	יִשְׂרָאֵל
will be great	יִתְגַּדַּל

ב
English	Hebrew
God's glory	כְּבוֹדוֹ
bend the knee	כּוֹרְעִים
as it is written	כַּכָּתוּב
all	כָּל
all of us as one	כֻּלָּנוּ כְּאֶחָד
like You	כָּמוֹךָ

ל
English	Hebrew
to God	לַאֲדוֹן
Leah	לֵאָה
your heart	לְבָבְךָ
to bless	לְבָרֵךְ
from generation to generation	לְדוֹר וָדוֹר
lulav	לוּלָב
bread	לֶחֶם
(of the) going out from Egypt	(לְ)יְצִיאַת מִצְרַיִם
for honor	לְכָבוֹד
(of the) work of creation	(לְ)מַעֲשֵׂה בְרֵאשִׁית
to us	לָנוּ
forever and ever	לְעוֹלָם וָעֶד
to God's people	לְעַמּוֹ
to engage	לַעֲסוֹק
before	לִפְנֵי
to affix	לִקְבֹּעַ
to praise	לְשַׁבֵּחַ
to hear	לִשְׁמֹעַ

מ
English	Hebrew
happy	מְאַשֵּׁר
what [is]	מַה
thank, give thanks (boy/man)	מוֹדֶה
thank, give thanks (girl/woman)	מוֹדָה
thank (plural)	מוֹדִים
our Savior	מוֹשִׁיעֵנוּ
mezuzah	מְזוּזָה

English	Hebrew
and will be holy	וְיִתְקַדַּשׁ
and night	וְלַיְלָה
and shield	וּמָגֵן
and rescuer	וּמוֹשִׁיעַ
and it is said	וְנֶאֱמַר
and exalted	וְנִשָּׂא
and gave (and giving)	וְנָתַן
and for, and on	וְעַל
and righteousness (justice)	וָצֶדֶק
and commands us	וְצִוָּנוּ
and mercy	וְרַחֲמִים

ז
English	Hebrew
memory	זֵכֶר
memory	זִכָּרוֹן

ח
English	Hebrew
renew	חַדֵּשׁ
everyday	חוֹל
walls	חוֹמוֹת
living, lives	חַי
life	חַיִּים
Hanukkah	חֲנֻכָּה
kindness	חֶסֶד
acts of loving-kindness	חֲסָדִים טוֹבִים
darkness	חֹשֶׁךְ

ט
English	Hebrew
good	טוֹב
(God's) goodness	טוּבוֹ
good	טוֹבִים

י
English	Hebrew
Your hands	יָדֶיךָ
(God) will be	יִהְיֶה
(let us) praise	יְהַלְלוּ
Adonai	יְיָ
our days	יָמֵינוּ
will rule	יִמְלֹךְ
Jacob	יַעֲקֹב
will make	יַעֲשֶׂה
Isaac	יִצְחָק

Your people	עַמְּךָ
tree	עֵץ
tree of life	עֵץ חַיִּים
evening	עֶרֶב
makes	עֹשֶׂה

פ

wonder(s)	פֶּלֶא
Your face	פָּנֶיךָ
fruit(s)	פְּרִי, פֵּרוֹת

צ

rock	צוּר
Zion, Israel	צִיּוֹן

ק

holiness, Kiddush	קִדּוּשׁ
holiness	קְדוּשָׁה
holy	קֹדֶשׁ
makes us holy	קִדְּשָׁנוּ
sound, voice	קוֹל

ר

great	רַב
Rebecca	רִבְקָה
Rachel	רָחֵל

שׁ

shofar	שׁוֹפָר
grant, put	שִׂים
peace, hello, good-bye	שָׁלוֹם
peace in the home	שְׁלוֹם בַּיִת
peace	שְׁלָמָא
name	שֵׁם
set, put	שָׂם
God's name	שְׁמֵהּ
(God's) name, his name	שְׁמוֹ
Your name, your name (to a boy or man)	שִׁמְךָ
hear	שְׁמַע
who gave, that gave	שֶׁנָּתַן
Sarah	שָׂרָה

ת

praise	תְּהִלָּה
splendor, praises	תְּהִלֹּת
Torah	תּוֹרָה
Torah of	תּוֹרַת
God's Torah	תּוֹרָתוֹ
the Torah of life	תּוֹרַת חַיִּים
forever	תָּמִיד
shall go forth	תֵּצֵא